THE HOTEL OF DREAMS

THE HOTEL OF DREAMS
AND OTHER STORIES

JOHN LUCAS

All rights reserved. No part of this work covered by the copyright herein may be reproduced or used in any means – graphic, electronic, or mechanical, including copying, recording, taping, or information storage and retrieval systems – without written permission of the publisher.

Printed by imprintdigital
Upton Pyne, Exeter
www.digital.imprint.co.uk

Typesetting and cover design by narrator
www.narrator.me.uk
info@narrator.me.uk
033 022 300 39

1st edition, 2018
Published by Plas Gwyn Books

2nd edition, 2019
Published by Shoestring Press
19 Devonshire Avenue, Beeston, Nottingham, NG9 1BS
(0115) 925 1827
www.shoestringpress.co.uk

© Copyright: John Lucas
© Cover photography by Denny Müller on Unsplash

The moral right of the author has been asserted.

ISBN 978-1-912524-27-3

For Graham Lester George

> What sap
> went through that little thread
> to make the cherry red!
>
> – Marianne Moore

CONTENTS

Prefatory Note	1
Who Killed Gaitskell	3
Riddance	19
The Nature of Gothic	35
A is for….	53
Water	75
It's None of Your Business	81
To Avoid Those Eyes	87
The Goods	91
The Furies	101
In the Sweat of Thy Face	113
The First Time	131
So We Beat on	139
Fish and Beans	145
The Hotel of Dreams	157

Prefatory Note

The stories included in the following pages were written at different times of my life. Some were published in journals, most of which have long since gone out of existence, others first appeared in compilations of short fiction. All will, I hope, give pleasure to readers encountering them here for the first time.

John Lucas

Who Killed Gaitskell

"So that's another of them," David said.

We were finishing breakfast, at least I was. David as usual had the newspaper drooping open in front of him, the toast I'd buttered and arranged in triangles on his plate still untouched, while a corner of the paper rested in the bowl of jam he claimed especially to like, blackberry, the first of the season.

"Your toast will be cold," I said. Then, as a hand came out to feel for the plate and draw it toward him—a frill of butter was now added to the bottom of the page—I said, "Who? What?"

I could hear the crack of his jaws as he munched, but when he spoke—a single word—it was so muffled that I could make nothing of it. I stood, cleared the table, and went to lean over his dressing-gowned shoulder.

Tilting slightly away from me, he pointed to the obituary he was reading.

"Bernard Lovell?"

David turned and glanced up at me. Why so surprised, his look said. I peered at the details given at the foot of the obituary. *Alfred Charles Bernard Lovell, radio astronomer and physicist, born 31 August 1913; died 6 August 2012.* "He was 98," I said, uncertain whether to be more impressed than shocked. "I thought he'd been dead for years."

"He would have been if the Russians had had their way."

"What?"

"*Apparently* they tried to poison him." He turned back to the newspaper and I read the words he was pointing to.

"As the man behind the giant telescope at Jodrell Bank, Sir Bernard was a pioneer of radio astronomy and the study of cosmic rays. When the telescope tracked Sputnik, the world's first satellite that was launched by the Soviets, the communist regime became very interested in Sir Bernard. In 1963 they invited him to the USSR for an unprecedented tour of their observatories. Soon after, he fell ill with severe sickness and remained so for a month. It would be another 46 years before he voiced his suspicion as to the cause, but when he did, in a television interview in 2009, jaws dropped in astonishment: the Soviets, he said, had tried to kill him by bombarding him with lethal radiation."

I paused in my reading. "David," I said, "do you believe this? I mean, 46 years later, a very old man…. Could his mind have been wandering, do you think?"

David rammed the remains of his toast into his mouth. When he could speak again, he said "Read on."

So I did.

"*He also hinted that the KGB had tried to 'turn' him during his visit, implying that his refusal to defect would have given them another reason to want him dead.*"

David tilted his head, his eyes meeting mine with that familiar sceptical, quizzical, gaze.

"So the KGB tried to do for poor Bernard Lovell?"

"Or the CIA," David said, smiling more to himself than to me. He pushed back his chair, got slowly to his feet, then dropped the roughly folded newspaper beside his chair before leaving the kitchen.

Yes, that was what both look and smile meant. They always did. Conspiracy. If one side is accused then the other side has scored a victory. Agents, double agents. Vodka Cola. David was a conspiracy theorist. Should X be accused of committing murder you can be sure that Y is the guilty party.

After I had stacked the dishwasher and while David was upstairs showering and getting dressed, I sat at the now cleared table, and picked up the newspaper, intending to read the obituary for myself. But I did no more than glance at it. Instead,

I found myself remembering how in my girlhood Lovell's name, along with that of Fred Hoyle, held an almost mystical power over me. *Hoyle and Lovell.* The way to the stars. I'd even borrowed from the school library Hoyle's book, *The Frontiers of Astronomy*, urged to do so by my chemistry teacher, a man who told us that new worlds were opening and that we would be in the vanguard of the coming revolution. 1957 that was, the year of Sputnik, which, the teacher explained, was Russian for "fellow-traveller," adding that Yuri Gagarin, the first man in space, was a harbinger of the new, expanding universe, and that his voyage showed what could be accomplished by advanced societies who'd waved goodbye to superstition and understood that the future good of the World (he managed to imply a capital letter) would depend on science, pure and applied. "Men in white collars will be replaced by men in white coats." That was one of his sayings. "Scientists are the friends of all humanity." That was another.

The teacher—Mr. Finlay—made no secret of his socialism. He wore red socks, a red tie, and at morning assembly left the platform before prayers began, pulling open both swing doors before exiting from the stuffy hall. One door would have been enough, but I suppose he wanted to introduce into our suburban lives as much fresh air as he possibly could. "We are not what we are but what we do." That came from Karl Marx, so Finlay told us. His pulling wide those grammar school doors was his way of showing that he was a friend to the expanding world of science.

I couldn't imagine being friendly with Finlay, though. I thought of those greasy, unwashed straggles of grey hair through which, as he bent over sinks and Bunsen-burners, you could see the blotchy wrinkles of his scalp, I remembered the care we took to keep out of range of his sewer breath. Besides, he didn't seem very good at chemistry. Experiments he demonstrated often went wrong, or didn't work at all. As someone muttered after one more of Finlay's failures to produce the right chemical reaction, if science is supposed to be the future, then the future isn't looking good. So I was glad when, at the end of our fourth year, he left. Our new teacher was a great improvement and for a while I seriously thought about joining the science sixth form, though in the end I allowed myself to be persuaded that I was better suited to modern languages.

But Finlay's belief in science, no matter how poor an advertisement he himself seemed for the world view he championed, stayed with me. Once, late one evening early in our marriage, a little silly on wine, and bantering with David about whether in the scale of things the Humanities or Natural Sciences mattered more, I warbled a pastiche version of the old Gershwin song. "Shakespeare may crumble and Descartes may tumble, they're only made of clay, But Hoyle and Lovell are here to stay."

Hoyle and Lovell.

Reading that obituary I must have said the names aloud, because when I looked up from the newspaper, my grey-haired husband stood in the doorway, eyebrow raised in mute enquiry.

Trying to ignore his look, pitched somewhere between amusement and cod-concern—has she finally lost her marbles—I said, "Why are you dressed for going out?"

"Because 'out' is where we're going."

"Not yet, surely. They're expecting us for lunch, not mid-morning coffee." And then, as he opened his mouth to speak again, I realised with a rush of pleasure that he'd accepted my suggestion.

"I'll go and get ready," I said. And as I passed him, I reached out to touch his arm.

"Thanks," I said, "it won't take us far out of our way, I promise."

"It had better not," David said.

The previous evening over dinner I'd shown him Pevsner's entry on a church that lay between us and the Colstones. "A gem." So, anyway, a local friend had assured me. "Vindows vith stained-glass fragments of unusual extent and completeness, as vell as a font vith richly crocketed gables." David read out the words in a Herr Doktorish voice when I pushed the book over to him. "You vish to go inspect, nein?" Then, dropping back into his own voice, "traipsing around another uninteresting bit of Olde England that's a good mile off our route. Can't see the point. Anyway, the place will almost certainly be locked."

So his giving in to my wish to look the church over was enough, as my mother would have said, to put a spring in my step, and as we left the house I stretched up and kissed him on his half-averted cheek.

***

The church was locked. A scrap of paper pinned to the heavy oak door told us that anyone desirous of inspecting the interior of St. Matthew's should contact a Mrs Braithwaite, either by phone (a number was given) or by calling in person at Rose Cottage, Cranmer Street.

"In person" David said, turning away as I made a forlorn, frustrated attempt with both hands to wrench round the handle's iron loop. "No point in sending the servant, then." To his credit, he said nothing about being proved right, though his small smile said "see, I knew we'd be wasting our time," and he allowed himself a joke, one I didn't follow, about the unfortunate conjunction of Rose and Cranmer.

Stepping out from the little porch into mild drizzle, we walked slowly round the "edifice," as David put it, keeping to the flagged path and breathing in the dank melancholy that seemed to sift down from rustily barred windows set too high in the grey stone for us to be able to see inside. We paused beside some gravestones looming among tall wet grasses and scrags of bush but failed to decipher names and dates on all but a few which iodine blotches of lichen and weathering had not yet made anonymous, then, having glanced up at the squat tower—"home to the moping owl" I said, hoping for a smile as I slipped my arm in his, but David merely grunted—we returned in silence to the car. The time of indulgence was over.

***

"Oh, *that* church," Geoff Colstone said, as he handed us glasses of sherry. Tall and cheery, his open-neck shirt and old corduroys making me and I suspect David feel over-dressed, he stood on the hearthrug of their large, square drawing-room, and when he raised his glass, David and I, perched on the old leather settee facing him, followed suit. "Can't say I've ever looked at it. Dunno about Geraldine, though. Must ask her."

"Ask me what? No, don't stand up."

But David, already on his feet, went over to where she stood, just inside the door, gripped her shoulders as if she were a prize exhibit at the Antiques Road Show, and said "You're looking remarkably bonny." Then, stooping, he kissed her.

Lucky for some, I thought. But it was true. My old friend *was* looking well. In her full-length pale blue dress that matched the colour of her eyes, the unguarded smile brightening her scarcely-lined face, abundant hair ghosting its former gold, you'd never have guessed that less than a year earlier chemotherapy had for a while changed her to near-skeletal thinness, nor that hair loss had caused her to wear a hat at all times—"As much against the cold as to safeguard my attractions" she said with a wry smile the first time I saw her after her treatment began.

Her husband, who was watching her with a look in which tender regard blended with tolerant amusement of David's gallantry, said, "Dillsthorpe Church. St Matthew's. Our guests found it locked against them. Know anything about it, Gerry?"

Geraldine came over to join me on the settee, leaving David and Geoff beside the hearth, from where the two of them could look across at us.

As she sat, she leant over to kiss me, and I breathed in the aroma of her scent—that lemony aroma I always associated with the cat-like grace of movement I knew men found so attractive. Looking at me before she turned back to Geoff, the smile playful but with some sharper meaning lurking within, she said, "Ruin bibbers, randy for antique."

"Eh?" Geoff was nonplussed.

"It's poetry, darling." She laughed openly then. "Not that you'd know. Any more than you'd know a rood screen from a reredos, now would you?"

He blinked and I thought he might have been offended by her words. But he answered lightly enough, "Beware or I shall recite 'Sea Fever'" Then, to me, "My party piece. Made me a finalist in the school's public speaking contest of 1956. And that, I can honestly say, is the only use poetry's ever been to me. I never heard yet that it helped to keep the world turning. How about you, David."

"Oh, I removed my shoulder from the wheel years ago," David said. "Now I vegetate and cogitate and try not to notice the world at all."

"If only that were true," I said, finishing my sherry.

He looked across at me, eyebrow raised as if to challenge my remark.

"The world is too much with us," I said, "even if Sir Bernard Lovell has now left the stage."

"Who?" Geoff asked, and Geraldine said vaguely "Oh, yes, he died recently, didn't he? Incredibly old."

"David thinks the KGB tried to poison him."

"*Really*." They spoke together, Geraldine agog, Geoff sceptical. Here we go, I could tell he was thinking, another of David's theories.

And as though she could read her husband's thoughts, Geraldine stood—I noticed she had to lever herself up rather carefully—and said, "I really only came in to tell everyone that lunch is ready. Shall we go through?"

***

We were past the soup and well into the main course, a kedgeree of smoked haddock with side salad of rocket and tomatoes—"Vegetables from our own garden" Geoff said a trifle smugly—before David, as I knew he would, brought the subject round to where he wanted it to be; though with, for him, some subtlety, he asked, momentarily downing tools while he propped his elbows on the table round which we sat, "If poetry doesn't keep the world turning, Geoffrey, you presumably put your trust in science, or scientists?"

"Geoffrey." David never used the diminutive, honouring the fact that the men were ancillaries in a friendship which for Geraldine and me went back some fifty years. Fresh from school, mine in the Midlands, hers in London, we'd met as first-year students at Manchester, and what at first seemed no more than a passing acquaintanceship gradually deepened into a life-long affection. David and Geoff were therefore, as one of them, I can't remember who, said, "friends by marriage." But they got along well enough, though David was, I knew, uneasy at what he took to be Geoff's polite but scarcely concealed quizzicality about his work. In Geoff's view teachers had little understanding of "the real world." That, anyway, was what David claimed, and although I never heard Geoff say as much, there was, I had to admit, some justification for David's assumption. The guarded "really" with which Geoff had met the suggestion of Lovell's poisoning was typical of a certain edginess between the two men, mostly sheathed but always ready to gleam out.

Perhaps for that reason our friendship had certain bounds set to it, quite apart from the fact that the Colstones lived in one of the wealthier London suburbs—Geoff was a city banker—whereas after a few years of wandering from teaching post to post around the north we fetched up back in the Midlands. But with Geoff's retirement and their decision to retire to "the country," which in their case meant a substantial Georgian house in a village not far from us, we began to see more of each other, and turn and turn-about lunch had become a monthly ritual.

I'd have been happy to meet more frequently, but David chafed at what he always said was the opportunity table talk gave the two Gs, as he called them, to show off. "How many sentences will it take to get from the weather to Peter Perfect," he said once, as we waited for them to arrive. "The book's open and I'm laying good odds on five." Their only child, Peter, who had been to public school, was now, so we were given to understand, an important link in the chain of command at Coutts.

But I didn't mind. I could share with Geraldine my worries about Helen's first, difficult pregnancy, and she understood my feelings when, soon after Cathy's marriage to Mark, she went off with him to live in Sydney.

"*Sadly?*" Geoff was genuinely astonished when I passed on the news of our younger daughter's imminent departure. "Sydney, let me tell you, Jo, is one of the great cities of the world. I only wish I had a child of mine living there. I'd be back and forth from one year's end to the next."

"Easy for him to talk," David said when they'd left. "He could probably buy his own jet if he wanted to."

So there was the slight but unmistakeable glint, a steely regard, when, on this first, supposedly celebratory lunch for the four of us since the official pronouncement of Geraldine's being free of cancer, he challenged Geoff to say whether he put his trust in scientists. He had something to prove.

Geoff took some time before replying. He tapped a finger against the bottle of Chablis that stood at his elbow, and, with a slight shrug, as though to dislodge some irritant caught between his shoulder blades, said, "Render unto Caesar would be my way of putting it."

"What does that mean?"

Still looking into his wine glass, Geoff said, "That we have a good deal to thank the men in white coats for." His voice was studiously neutral.

I said, "That's more or less what a science teacher at school used to tell us."

Geoff bowed his head in pretend humility. "I make no pretence to originality." Then, perhaps hoping to put an end to the subject, "More wine, anyone?"

But David wasn't to be deflected. "I'm with you, as it happens. I mean, I can't imagine anyone, anyone in power that is, wanting to poison a poet. Or for that matter kill him by any other means."

"I can," Geraldine said at once. "Salman Rushdie."

"Strictly speaking he's not a poet," I said, smiling at her, but David waved my words aside.

"Point taken," he said to Geraldine. After which he paused and drank from his refilled glass. "I should have said that I can't imagine anyone wanting *secretly* to kill a writer. I mean, the loonies who were out to get Rushdie made no bones about it, did they? They trumpeted their *fatwah* from the roof tops."

"Or minarets," Geoff said. He passed his plate to Geraldine. "Any chance of a second helping?" Then, to David, "So you think the KGB tried secretly to snuff out this man Lovell?"

"No," David said, "that's what *he* thought."

"Lordy." Geoff shook his head. "This is getting too deep for me."

And Geraldine, handing Geoff his refilled plate, said, "But the KGB do that kind of thing, don't they? That man—what was his name—the one they followed over to London a few years ago…"

"Litvinenko," David said, a touch brusquely. "Of course they got rid of him. *Everyone* knows that. Polonium in his tea. Probably what was on the umbrella tip that did for Georgi Markov."

"The man at the bus stop," I said in answer to Geraldine's puzzled look. "But that was before the Cold War came to an end. It was different then."

"Yes, yes." David laid a hand on my arm. I was being corrected. "But Litvinenko was an enemy of the state. He'd been handing information to M15. It was still the Cold War as far as the Russians were concerned. And it still is."

"Bulgarian, actually," Geoff murmured. "Markov was a Bulgarian."

"Same difference," David said.

Geraldine said, "I don't quite see where this is all leading?" looking as though for reassurance across at Geoff, who, lips pursed, shook his head slightly at her, a gesture David missed.

Frowning down at his upturned hands, an expression I knew all too well, he said, slowly, "Bluff and double bluff. Suppose Lovell was actually poisoned by the CIA? Or by M15 acting for the CIA?" His head came up as he glanced around and, yes, there was the smile, measured, knowing, a smile that said 'endgame. Now get out of *that* if you can.' And he shook his head when, silently, Geraldine mimed the offer of more kedgeree.

"You're suggesting that they tried to kill one of their own top scientists, the man who tracked sputnik?"

Still smiling, David studied the look of incredulity on Geoff's face. "Ah, so you know about that," he finally said. "But they didn't kill him, did they?" Now the hands were reversed and pressed onto the table. Game over. "And there's the difference between what happened to Lovell and what happened to Markov and Litvinenko. If the KGB are out to get you, they kill you. But Lovell didn't die." He paused. "Any more than Tony Benn did."

"Tony Benn?" Standing to clear the plates, Geraldine was stopped, open-mouthed. "What's *he* got to do with this?"

"He was poisoned," David looked smilingly at her. "Didn't you know that?"

She stared at him, uncertain whether he was joking. "No," she said, and it was as though she was telling David not to be silly. Blushing faintly at her perceived rudeness, she asked her husband, "Have *you* heard about this, Geoff?"

Geoff looked at David, nodded, then, to her, "There was a time in Benn's ministerial life when he got the shakes," he said.

"Well, given the amount politicians are said to drink I'd not be surprised if most of them have got the shakes."

"Tony Benn is a teetotaller." David smiled tolerantly at Geraldine. Fancy not knowing that.

"And a self-righteous, humourless pain in the bum," Geoff said.

"Even if that were true, which I happen to think it isn't, it hardly constitutes a reason to poison him."

"If he'd had his way he'd have wrecked this country."

"Ah." David nodded as though he'd proved his point, "so it's alright for a minister of state to be assassinated by the CIA?"

Geraldine was still hovering beside the door, tray-laden, but now she said with determined brightness, "Shall we all have some coffee? To go with the Stilton. Geoff drove over to Cropwell Bishop, especially."

"That was kind of you," I said to Geoff, watching as his wife began to manoeuvre herself and the stacked tray through the door.

I rose to help her, but "No," she said, "I can manage on my own. You stay and entertain the men." And she winked at me. Keep the peace, she meant.

"David loves Stilton, don't you," I said brightly.

But he wouldn't look at me. Instead, he went on staring at Geoff, waiting for him to answer.

And eventually Geoff did. "By your own reckoning," and his voice hinted at the disdain I knew would infuriate David, "if Benn had died then it would have meant that the KGB were behind the dastardly deed. But because it was the CIA he was let off with a caution. Is that it?" He paused, then said into a silence that had become tense, "If so, I think he got off lightly."

"*Lightly!*" David, now leaning forward to stare across at Geoff, was momentarily disturbed when Geraldine reappeared and began to unload cups and saucers, followed by an impressive wheel of Stilton.

I made to move David's elbow in order to put a plate in front of him, but he shook off my hand, then slammed his own down on the polished rosewood, making the cups my old friend was attempting to set out rattle in their saucers.

Geoff was unfazed. He pushed the cheese-board over to David, watching as, hand trembling, David hacked out a wedge of Stilton, then said thoughtfully, "If you're right, then Lovell was being used to advertise the evils of communism by agents who might have ended up poisoning the very man they needed in order to keep tabs on the enemy. One slip and they could have killed him. He was certainly very ill. Whereas Benn had a dose of the trembles. So yes, even if the CIA was behind that, I think Wedgie got off lightly."

There was a pause while Geraldine poured us all coffee.

Looking at David's bent head—he was using a forefinger to trap some crumbs of Stilton, almost as though he'd given up on the topic he'd started and now wanted to concentrate on his cheese—Geoff said, his voice coaxing David to look up, "Don't you think you're ascribing more ability and judgement to our friendly CIA operatives than they deserve? They couldn't even get Castro's beard to fall out." And he smiled, first at me, then his wife.

David kept his head down. Geoff made a theatrical show of slapping his forehead with his free hand. "Oh, *of course*. Poisoning his cigars was a KGB trick to discredit their opposite number. They even managed to lay off spiking the tobacco with too much cyanide or polonium or whatever." And he leant back in his chair, arms folded. "Devilish clever, these Russkies," he said.

I laughed. I couldn't help myself. So, as David's head came up and he stared around at us all, a slow smile lightening his expression, did Geraldine; and her laugh, I guess, was one of relief. Friendly relations had been restored.

Finally, briefly, David joined in the laughter.

For a few minutes neither man interrupted as Geraldine and I were allowed to discuss our children and related matters.

But we were all watching when, having cleared his plate and emptied his cup, David said, "You're probably right, Geoffrey."

I glanced at my watch. Soon we could be on our way. Let the meal end in peace, please, I thought.

"So which side do you reckon killed Gaitskell?"

Without losing his affable smile, Geoff said, "Neither. Gaitskell died of natural causes."

"A viral illness that no specialist could prevent from killing him?"

"It happens."

"I don't believe that."

"Now why doesn't that surprise me?"

"Perhaps because you prefer to believe the lies spread about by those in power. It makes for a cosier view of the world."

"Oh, for Christ's sake," Geoff said, the smile no longer evident, unfolding his arms and spreading them wide, palms upward in a gesture of weary exasperation. "You're now going to tell me that the hero of Socialism was bumped off by the CIA."

"Unless it was the KGB who feared that he was a cold war warrior. Gaitskell was all for Britain staying in the arms race."

"And Wilson was in Moscow's pay. Isn't that what the CIA believed?"

Face flushed, David made a show of waving away Geoff's words.

"Disinformation," he said. "Only fools would believe that."

"And being fools, it never occurred to the KGB to poison Wilson's HP sauce. Or spike his Wincarnis."

"David, we should think about leaving."

I pushed back my chair and stood, meeting Geraldine's eyes as I did so, sensing rather than seeing the tiny, rueful shrug that went with her grateful smile.

A few minutes later, after awkward handshakes between the men watched over by my friend and me, and after we'd hugged each other and she'd whispered in my ear words that might have been *never mind*, we were on our way down their long drive, having agreed that the next lunch date would be at our house, and all too aware of the door being shut firmly behind us.

***

For the first twenty minutes of the journey home, wet from rain that had fallen on us as we made for the car, neither of us spoke. I forced myself to concentrate on keeping a good distance from the traffic ahead, watching through the *tick, tick, tick* of the wipers for any sign of cars slowing down, trying to focus on the ruby glow of brake-lights.

I could sense rather than see David clenching and unclenching his fists, hear the occasional hiss of his breath.

But at last words burst from him. "Condescending bastard." Then, "For God's sake, if you're going to slow down you might at least change gear."

There was a lay-by a little ahead. I signalled and turned into it, stopping the car abruptly.

"What the hell are you doing?" His voice was thick with rage and probably too much of Geoff's expensive wine.

Keeping my own voice as steady as I could, I began, "David..." I took a breath, waited for my heart to stop pounding, and tried again. "The reason I'm driving this car," I said when I had control of my voice, "is because you're over the limit. I don't *like* driving the bloody thing, not in the rain, and especially not with you in the passenger seat ready to criticise every and any move I make." I paused. "I like even less your spoiling what was meant to be a special occasion for *my* friend," I said, aware of the sudden thickness in my own throat.

Knuckling my hand I began to scour the fogged windscreen. "Least of all," I said, determined to speak slowly, "do I enjoy being treated as someone too innocent, for which read too stupid, to penetrate the murky underworld of international politics which your mighty brain alone can illuminate. In fact I *hate* it. Condescending bastard."

After which we sat there, staring through clouded glass at the puddled, empty lay-by, aware of discarded paper cartons fluttering along its verge like wounded birds in the teeming rain. Two or three cars went past, the passenger in one turning to look back at the couple who were, surely, far too old to be adulterous lovers snatching half an hour of fugitive passion before returning to the stale routines of domesticity.

Eventually, David said, "I see. Well, I'm sorry, but I think these things matter."

He wasn't sorry at all. He never was. He never would be. But still, he was my husband. And he had allowed me that wasted visit to St. Matthew's. And he was also right about Geoff. It had required the two of them to wreck the occasion to which my old friend and I had been so looking forward, and between them they'd made a thorough job of it, Geoff with his man-of-the-world smugness, David with his suppressed bitterness. And what made it worse was that I knew I could never talk to him about any of this. It would have to go unacknowledged, his sour awareness of a life running to seed, his recognition that to most people his claims to understand the world's devious ways were merely the delusions of an undistinguished teacher with an inflated sense of self-worth. I couldn't even tell him I was sorry—not for me, but for him.

I turned the key in the ignition, waited for a twelve-wheeler to pass, eased cautiously out into the speeding traffic, and we finished our journey, as we'd begun it, in silence.

Riddance

Hello Poplar Street, pleased to see me? Brief pause while you consider the question. OK. Time's up. I'll take that for a No, then. No bunting, no *Welcome Home Stranger* signs. In fact, and not to put too fine a point on it, nothing, *niet*, *nada*, not a sausage, as my old gran used to say. But then to be fair you didn't know I'd be coming, did you? For some reason or other I failed to give you advance notice of my movements. No chance then for the Mayor and Corporation to provide an official greeting. No red carpet. Brass band not on parade. Har. Har.

Alright, next question. What's new? Nothing much, I'm guessing. A fake-Georgian front door at No.2 that I certainly don't recall, probably painted maroon though in the dark it's difficult to tell, and surely I'd have remembered that poncey carriage lamp at No.8, but for the rest we have a steady-state street of terraced houses that belong to an anyhow town with what even estate agents would be hard put not to call pocket-handkerchief front gardens, protected though they are from the public highway by miniature picket fences or step-over privet. An oasis of calm in an ever-shifting world. Oh, very droll. Haut amusant. That's Poplar Street for you. Not a poplar to be seen, of course, nor any other tree for that matter. Nothing for one of our feathered friends to claim as home territory. No change there, then.

Right. Time to abandon this riotous attempt at jocularity. Time to confront the past.

The fanlight over the door of No.17 was illumined. She, or whoever lived there now, must be in. Or was the light on simply to fool would-be burglars? At half-past seven o'clock of a winter's evening? I don't think so, sarge.

So, what next? At his back was No.24, where the Macauleys had lived for ever and a day and, if they *were* still "in residence"—their term of choice—and clinging to their bible-and-never-on-Sunday- or-any-other-day existence, would certainly recognise him, so no to that. No.26 then? One of the re-decorated houses, that fake stone cladding under the street lamp's uncertain glow looking decidedly recent, suggested new occupancy.

He could try there. But what to say? "I have a parcel for a Mrs Bevan at No.17. Can't get an answer, any idea where she might be?" Spot the flaws with that, if you will. You have two minutes and be sure to give valid reasons for your conclusions. OK. Quite apart from the fact that recent incomers might not know her, there was the slight problem that the small zip-up bag he was carrying didn't look much like a parcel. Besides which, why would anyone be delivering a parcel at that time of night? Besides which, a parcel deliverer ought to be wearing uniform or have some means of identification about his person. Besides which, she might well have changed her name. OK. Full marks.

Hello, the light's gone off.

He bent to tie an imaginary shoe-lace. The street lamp showed the figure of a man opening the gate of No.17, almost opposite from where he crouched. Not someone he recognised. So she'd sold up, moved away. He'd been misinformed.

But wait. We are not yet done. He's waiting for someone.

Tall, broad-shouldered, wearing what looked to be a donkey-jacket, the man held the gate open while another, slighter, figure emerged from the house and turned to pull the door firmly shut before, heels clacking on the slabbed path, she hurried to join him.

Yup, that's her, alright. And with a new bloke, I'm guessing.

Spot on, sarge. You will have observed that she's slotted her arm through his. Love's middle-aged dream.

He watched the pair walk briskly, laughing together, along the street and then turn the corner in the opposite direction from the one that minutes earlier had brought him here.

Wonder where they can be going? No basket, not that I can see. So, chances are they're not off to do some late-night shopping. A drink at the *Star* perhaps, at all events not the *Three Bargees*. Certainly not there. Bad vibes. But still, thank you, God. Fifteen minutes is all I need.

From further up the street came the sounds of some rubbish music, howl and thud, leaking from a bedroom window. But no one creeping on the sidewalk. Poplar Street was empty. Poplar but not popular. Right. Over we go.

Four strides and he was at the front door. The key went in, turned. So she hadn't changed the lock.

Once inside, he shut the door softly behind him, decided against putting the chain across.

Back propped against the door, he breathed out slowly, waited for his heart rate to slow.

So, having effected an entry, let's have a butcher's. Cast our beadies around us, as I doubt anyone ever said.

Hallway's as per, I see. Coil matting, the same framed reproductions hanging on what may be re-painted white walls—*The Hay Wain, The Fighting Temeraire*—and the stripped pine doors, including that half-opened one on the left through which I am not going to peer in order to see whether she's still got the dark grey three-piece suite and the drinks cabinet, though I regret to say that I can't help noticing at the hall's far end the kitchen door, shut now, which retains the stupid metal plaque he screwed to it years ago. *Gourmet Delights*. Tell me about them.

OK. Upstairs.

Upstairs seemed the same, too. Dark brown carpet on the landing, yup, white paper lampshade, cream walls, perhaps re-painted like the hall, wouldn't you say, sarge, but definitely the same colour as I remember from years past. Some things never change. And here, aha, aha, what he'd come for.

Still hanging above his own old bedroom door, the box-room it used to be called, was the small, rusting anchor he'd found wandering along the shore-line on their first real family holiday, surprisingly heavy when lifted, far too heavy for a small boy to carry, but retrieved by doting parents from the rock-pool where he'd seen it lying, and brought home in the boot of their old and battered Ford; after which, the worst of the rust having been scraped away, his father, who was good with his hands, and we can say *that* again, put up the narrow shelf over the door lintel before lifting the object into position.

A boy's pride and delight in seeing the anchor up there, above *his* door. Pride and delight in showing it to a few school friends. And as though to confirm the pride of ownership, dear old dad, God bless him, had even tacked a metal strip of identification to the shelf's outer edge. *Found by Stephen, Littlehampton, July, 1981. "Home is our Anchor."* That, too, remained.

Yes, right.

He stood there, looking up at it. No tears, no fuss.

A few moments later he pushed open the main bedroom door, paused, holding his breath, then tiptoed in. Old habits die hard. You weren't supposed to enter your parents' bedroom.

A couple of dresses were draped over a cane chair, but he didn't want to look, nor at the man's cord trousers that lay on the floor beside them.

Standing in front of the dressing table, he saw the unframed photograph propped against the mirror. Himself in younger, but post-anchor days: on holiday at a different seaside resort, Weston-Super-Mare wasn't it, leaning up against a low promenade wall in black T-shirt and jeans, arms folded across his chest, the scowl barely kosher, more by way of pose. You're only young once. She'd taken the snap. They were on their own by then. And there, too, under the table's glass top, the one he'd posed for with college friends. At the end of his second year, that was. There never was a third.

He turned away, stood by the bed, pressed a hand against the candlewick bedspread, sat, paused for a moment then swung his legs up, lay full-length, hands clasped behind his head.

It had been a long, long day.

***

What's that?

He came to, listened, body taut, lower lip gripped by upper teeth.

Sod. Buggeration.

Someone was downstairs. Had they just returned?

Clatter of saucepans. A burst of laughter followed by applause, raised voices. Not TV. She wouldn't allow TV in the kitchen. Some radio discussion, then.

Bloody hell, what's *that* noise now?

Oh, yes. He let out his breath. The judder of water pipes.

He sneaked a look at his watch. Only just gone 8pm. They couldn't have been to a pub, then. A carry-out? Here's hoping. Perhaps they were settling down to eat, get the beauty of it 'ot. If so he might be able to creep downstairs and be out of the house before they noticed his presence. Let's be lucky.

OK. Action.

He sat up.

Fuck.

He'd not noticed the shelf above the bed.

Sod, oh *sod*. They *must* have heard the noise.

But no, no new sounds from downstairs, nothing to suggest they'd been alerted by his involuntary cry. Well, thank you, radio. Police warn that Discussion Programmes which keep their audiences enthralled are Prime Time for domestic burglaries.

Or was that someone on the stairs?

Was it…?

No, it was his own breath whispering in his ears.

Levering himself off the bed, he tiptoed across to the door, opened it

—And there she was, staring at him.

Anger in her look, and a sardonic twist of the lips.

But not surprised. Not that.

"Funny, we wondered if you'd try it on," she said.

He opened his mouth to speak but shut it without saying a word.

"What have you been doing?"

She peered round him and at the bed. "Sleeping? Hardly the sleep of the just, is it?" Her level look challenged him to speak.

Go on, say something.

We? We wondered? But no, he couldn't. He stood, silent, dared to look at her.

She was older, of course, but still attractive, and though the creases round her eyes were deeper now, her hair, the same curled, chestnut brown, framed her oval face, the wide lips, slightly flattened nose, rounded chin.

"All the way from Manchester, I suppose. With a rail warrant. If they still have them."

He nodded, mouth dry. Unable to speak, he took in her dark blue sweater and jeans, what had to be black leather boots, and now, when he raised his eyes, he saw that her gaze had softened, a little.

"You'd better come down," she said.

Turning, she led the way.

Careful not to let his heavy grip thump against the banisters, he followed her downstairs, along the hall, a small boy again, being taken to receive his punishment against arbitrary, unjust rules.

In the kitchen a man, dark-skinned, maybe a year or so younger than she was, stood beside the stove, one that had to be new, stirring the contents of a stainless steel saucepan. He looked over his shoulder, nodded, but said nothing. Under his short-sleeved grey T-shirt his body was lean, well-muscled.

She gestured to a chair beside the scrubbed wood table on which were piled a heap of groceries, tins, packets, some in cellophane wraps.

"Sit down." There was little warmth in the command.

He sat.

The man at the stove, transferring the spatula to his left hand, reached over and held out his right hand. "I'm Cobham," he said. The voice was level, easy. "Want a drink? Coffee, tea? Wine?"

"Nothing," he managed to say, releasing his hand from the other's grip. "Thanks." Then, "Cobham? What's your first name?"

"That *is* his first name."

"And you're Stephen." The man's smile was part quizzical, part sardonic. "Your mum said you might try to make it back here."

"Why?" he asked her. "I mean why did you think I'd come?"

"Intuition," she said, sitting down opposite him. Then, shrugging, "I don't know."

He wanted to say that until this morning he'd had no plans to return, especially in view of the fact that at no time during the past four years had she given him any hint of wanting him back, and that anyway he was a big boy now. But he held his peace.

Cobham turned back to the stove and said, over his shoulder. "Not necessarily a good idea, man. The police would see it at least as a case of breaking and entering."

"What have the police got to do with it?"

"We called them," she said.

He was shocked. "Well, call them back, say it was a mistake."

"It wasn't."

"This is crazy." He looked from one to the other of them. "Anyway, I didn't break in. I had a key."

"A *key*?" She stared at him, apprehensive. "You're not entitled to a key, you know that as well as I do." She paused, gave him a chance to reply, then added, "Or had you forgotten?"

"If you called the cops why offer me a drink?" he asked. "To keep me here until they arrive? To get me banged up again?" Anger surged within him, he knew himself to be sweating, could feel the blood throb at his temples.

"Cool it, man," Cobham spoke the words evenly, his accent London-based, well, southern. "They said they'd be here as soon as they could. That gives you another ten minutes."

He saw the look that passed from man to woman, the slight shake of head, the raised eyebrow. So the police hadn't been called. She wouldn't do that. Would she?

"I'll go as soon as you tell me about my father," he said to her. "Where he is? Tell me and I'll go."

She had gone over to stand beside the man, slid her arm round his waist, and her head was pressed against his shoulder.

"Is that why you came? To find out where that—where *he* is?" The look she directed at him was sceptical, disbelieving.

He nodded. The lies we tell.

"If you only knew how many times I've been asked that question." Her laugh was more a bark, but at least she seemed prepared to believe him. "Debt collectors, policemen, heavies in dark suits." She shook her head. "How should *I* know where he is. The only times I could guarantee where he was were the times he was behind bars."

"He's not there now, is he?"

"More's the pity," she said.

She came over to where he sat, leant over him, staring into his eyes as she said, slowly, "I know he's your father. He was once my husband." A pause, while she looked down at her hands, then raised her eyes to meet his. Her look was unwavering. Please understand, the look said, please don't be in any doubt, *please* believe me. "Stephen, I never want to see him again, *ever*. And I don't want to hear his name mentioned. He's done enough harm to last me several lifetimes. Enough harm to you, too."

Then she went back to join Cobham, who nuzzled the top of her head with his chin, moved his free hand lightly up and down her back, all the while stirring the contents of the saucepan.

"See, I'm happy now," she said, still looking steadily at her son, though this time there was a slight curve of the lips and, in her eyes, something that might have been a compassing regard.

He stood. "I'd better take myself off. Seeing that the police are on their way."

No response.

Again she was looking at him, her gaze travelling up and down his body, taking in his frayed jeans, the open-neck green shirt and pullover, dark brown cord jacket.

"You've lost weight." This time there was no mistaking the softening of tone.

"Yes, well, must be all that exercise I've been getting for the past years, plus plenty of healthy food." Ha, bloody ha.

"Do you need any money?"

"I'll be alright." He felt his throat tighten at the way she asked the question, the touch of her hand on his wrist.

He decided not to say goodbye to Cobham.

She followed him down the hallway. "I won't ask for the key back," she said, as she reached past him to pull open the front door.

He turned to face her.

"But you're supposed to ask for permission to visit," she said. "If you *do* want to come here again, phone first, check to make sure it's alright with us." The smile was reluctant, slow, not without a note of pleading. "Will you?"

Will I what? Phone? Come again?

There was a pause while she waited for him to speak, and, when he failed to do so, the smile went. "If you find your father, you can tell him from me that I'm OK, no thanks to him, and that's the way it's going to stay. Alright?"

"Alright."

But she hadn't finished. That single word seemed to have released her into speech. "Alright? Forging cheques. God, Stephen, what a fool. How the hell did you think you'd get away with that?" She was suddenly shaking with anger. "And why? *Why?*"

"You know why."

"I know I warned you against trying to help him."

He raised a hand in supplication. A plea for understanding. But he had to understand, too. And he did. Over the past years he'd had plenty of time to think about why that outbreak of uncontrollable, murderous rage which led to her calling the police had been a response not, as he'd claimed, to her refusal to help her husband, but to his own lost love for the father he'd tried so clumsily to help. And it was only when he threatened her that she used her earlier discovery of the forged cheques to get him put away. He was a danger to them both.

Standing on the doorstep of what used to be his home, he tried to think of usable words.

But before he could open his mouth, she said, "Well, we make our own beds." She sighed, her mouth turned down. "You let that bloody man make yours, and look where it got you."

He wanted to say, but didn't you ever love him? Didn't you? But the jut of her chin, the look in her eyes, stilled the words in his mouth.

He stepped through the door she held open for him, felt the sudden chill of night air and for the last time turned, wondering whether she might reach out to touch him, or whether he should try to touch her, shifted his bag from right to left hand, but, after looking levelly at him for a few moments she closed the door, and after that there was nothing for it but to turn and walk away.

***

The saloon bar of the *Bargees* was doing precious little business. The "No Smoking" sign must have driven most of its regular punters away, and how could so frowsty a pub hope to attract others? He was served by a bored-looking barman, new since his time, who kept one eye on the CCTV as he pulled the two pints of ale. Watching for possible car thieves. You're wasting your time, mate, Stephen thought. The real villain's here.

He carried one glass and his bag over to a table at the far end of the room, placed the glass in front of the man who sat there silent, and went back for his own pint.

Sitting opposite the man, who was looking at him in silent expectation, he took a sip of the beer without bothering to offer greetings.

"You took your time." The older man sat looking over the glass of beer he hadn't yet touched. "So, where is it?"

He shook his head, but didn't answer the question. Instead, "She doesn't want to see you," he said. "She's happy, got another man. Leave her alone."

"You mean you *talked* to her?" The voice was incredulous, on the verge of fury. "What the hell were you doing *talking* to her? You weren't supposed to be having some cosy meeting. I told you, if anyone's there, keep away."

"You also said that she's often out of an evening."

"So she is."

"Not *she*. *They*. Your informant slipped up there. Anyway, they came back sooner than I'd expected."

"What's his name?" The lips twisted in contempt. "No, let me guess. Jeremy? Quinton? Charles Chinless? Or has she gone all dyke? Is it Jemima I should be asking after? Queenie? Charlotte?" The laugh was rancorous.

"He's called Frank." No chance he'd give away his real name, nor his colour.

"And they caught you at it?" The scorn was accompanied by a grin of derision which changed to watchfulness. "You tell them anything?"

He laughed, scornful himself now. "No, I didn't tell them anything. I threw them off the scent. Thought my old dad would be proud of me the way I asked them, all blue-eyed innocence, if they had any idea where you were."

"And?"

"She said she didn't know, didn't want to know, and that she's happy." He paused. "And she is," he finally said.

His father looked at him, shook his bald head. "You always were a mother's boy," he said.

You bastard. But he didn't say the words and his attempted glare was met by an unwavering, half-amused look.

His father held out a hand, the sleeve of his black leather jacket riding up his bare, thin arm. "So, where is it? Let's have a looksee."

"Gone," Stephen said. "She must have chucked it out." He swallowed some beer, and, to avoid having to register his father's response, concentrated on the beer mat he was fiddling with. "Perhaps she didn't want to be reminded of earlier times."

Momentarily then, he looked up, met his father's grey-eyed stare behind which something stirred. Regret? No, not regret.

"Now why don't I believe that?"

He dared to say, "Why don't you go and see for yourself?"

His father ground the words out. "You know bloody well why not. Because If I got spotted it'd be me that was nabbed, not the bloody anchor."

"And if *I'd* been caught?"

His father grinned, the old, derisive twitch of the lips. "You were, remember."

"They could have turned me in." He decided not to mention his mother's bluff about having phoned the cops.

His father's shrug dismissed the possibility. "She wouldn't harm you. Whereas me…"

"Yes, she hates you, alright." Once more he lowered his gaze to the beer glass.

"Feeling's mutual. But father and son. Always a bond there."

Stephen glanced up, took in the mocking grin, turned his head to study unoccupied tables, chairs, flashing fruit machine, anything but accept the unbearable gaze of the father he'd once trusted, once, a long time ago, had loved, admired.

"Took some finding, you did." It was as if Stephen had been the thoughtless cause of his father's difficulties. "Good job your college kept in touch with you. That's what I call caring. Knew where you were, when you'd be coming out. Yes, very helpful they were. And very helpful *you* were, too, I admit. Once upon a time, that is. Not that it worked out as either of us might have hoped. Still, as the man says, that's life."

Father and son looked glancingly at each other and son was the first to crack. "You never apologised."

"Didn't I?" A hand was raised in mock confession. "Well, then. Sorry."

Ignore it. Keep your cool. Change the subject.

"Why did you *really* want that anchor?" he said.

The bald head came up from the hunched shoulders and his father leant further across the table so that Stephen saw in close-up the veiny, enamelled hardness of his eyes, their vitreous, corroded glitter. I don't know you, he thought, I haven't a clue who you are. Why ever did I think I could be related to you in any meaningful way, why was I prepared to do your bidding? Why? But he knew why. And when the other's words finally came, they seemed to scorch him so that he felt rather than heard them.

"I wanted to hurt her," his father said, speaking slowly, with flat, emphatic, almost didactic insistence. Teacher to dim pupil. "Make her feel unsafe. Since you ask, *that's* what I wanted." He sat back, smiling, lesson accomplished. But then he leant forward again. "Oh, yeh, and to let her know that the anchorless are free to go where they like. To do whatever they want. Like a rolling stone." The smile was now a rictus of arrogant disdain. "Will that do?"

So that was it. All the talk, all the reassurances, all the pretence of affection he'd laid on, all of it hogwash. He knew it had been, of course he knew, even though he'd tried to suppress the knowledge, had, for no matter how short a time earlier that day, wanted to believe his father. But, face it, want didn't equal hope. That morning, as the prison gates closed behind him and he saw and at once recognised the man waving to him from across the street, even then he'd felt less a jolt of pleasure than of apprehension. It reminded him all too clearly of that earlier moment, five years ago, when he'd seen the familiar figure waiting across the street as he emerged from a lecture hall, and of how, as they sat in a pub, father had pleaded with son, told him about the heavies who were threatening him—"They mean business, Stephen."

And now, when—*especially* when—he was treated to a slap-up breakfast—"something good to fill your belly with after all the porridge"—accompanied by a snickery laugh—Stephen sensed that the show of largesse wasn't mere contrition on top of paternal affection, that the stumbling, semi-articulate words intended to convey comfort were calculated, an act, especially as, once their plates were clean, his father let drop, casually, his proposal for how they could spend the day together, a trip they could take. "Down Memory Lane."

"Just you and me. I've got the tickets. No need to worry about paying me back." Mighty big of him.

But—"Derby, why Derby?" he'd asked, at once suspicious.

"Tell you on the train, you've got nowhere else to go, have you, no other plans?"

And no, he hadn't. "Well, then." And once they were settled into their seats facing each other in the half-empty carriage, his father had leant over to explain what he had in mind before handing over the house key he'd held on to "from the day she threw me out."

"I don't get it," Stephen had said, staring from key to his father and then back to the key. "What's the point?"

The train was slowing to a stop. Sheffield. Why don't I get out here, he wondered, tell him I want no part of this stupid scheme and take a train back to Manchester.

As though suspecting this, his father reached over, gripped his wrist. It was for both of them, he said. "You and me." A way of getting closer to each other, father and son, a sort of pact. "She treated you same as she did me. Shopped you soon as she cottoned on you'd been trying to help me"

"By raiding her bank account? That was your idea."

"Don't think I'm not grateful."

Now, as they faced each other in the pub, his father repeated the words. "Don't think I'm not grateful," he said. But as before there was no warmth in his voice, nor in the thin smile that came and went in an instant. "Oh, and I'll have the key back."

And now he *could* speak. "No, you won't," he said, laughing, in relief, released into a sudden light-headed pleasure at what he suddenly knew he would say next.

But it was his father who spoke first. "What do you mean?" Anger and, at the same time, consternation. Son daring to oppose father. This wasn't in the script.

"I've got rid of it."

"You've *what?*"

"You heard. I've got rid of it. Chucked it away. And I'll tell you another thing. Mum's new bloke. He's alright. He'd have you for breakfast and bin the rubbish bits. Which, come to think of it, means most of you."

Not witty, I realise, but cause for satisfaction all the same. I should have told you long ago that you're a waste of space. Anyway, that's it.

Aware that he was now grinning at the disbelieving stare of the man who sat facing him, hands clamped round his empty glass, their whitening knuckles, he gulped down his own beer in one long swallow, stood, picked up his bag and slowly, deliberately, buttoned his cord jacket. "But feel free to go round there, knock on the door, invite yourself in for a look around. He'll probably break every bone in your lousy body before she decides to call the cops."

He turned to go, but swung back, took one last look at the man who was his father. "You know," he said, "I used to wonder when I heard her call you a petty criminal. Petty? What did it mean? Well, now I know. Except you're not big enough to be petty. *Petty? You?* Dream on."

Then, nodding a silent farewell to the indifferent barman, he pushed his way through the glass doors and for a long moment stood in the pub's empty forecourt, letting himself be buffeted by the night wind.

Well, that's torn it, as they say in fiction. How to lose two parents within an hour. Misfortune, perhaps, but not carelessness. Got that one wrong, Oscar.

He pulled up his collar against the cold. Farewell Poplar Street. Goodnight Vienna. There is a world elsewhere. Anyway, there'd better be.

It was a few yards to the hump-back bridge at the side of the pub. Leaning against the shallow parapet, he reached into his jeans' pocket, stared for a moment at the sliver of metal that lay glimmering in the palm of his hand, then lobbed it into the canal's coal-black water.

And for my next trick.

He unzipped his bag, pulled out the anchor, and as it followed the key into the blackness below the bridge, listened out for the splash which, when it came, was no louder than a moorhen might make launching itself out from the safety of the reed-fringed bank.

All done and dusted, sarge.

His load lighter now, he began to walk toward the station.

The Nature of Gothic

In the town square two capped and black-suited old men were drowsing on a bench beneath the wide-spread plane tree. One of them, jerking his head up as the car rumbled past, began to raise a hand in greeting but then let it fall back over the hand clasping his walking stick.

Next moment the Fiesta was out again into the countryside.

"We'll need to make a right turn soon," Hugh said to Clare, studying the map that lay open across his knees.

"Don't you mean left?"

"No." Hugh shook his head, careful not to use any term of possessive endearment. "It has to be right." He peered through the insect-spattered windscreen. "There it is," he said. "That's the road we need."

Clare nodded, lips pursed in a wry smile, and swung the car left onto the poplar-lined road, very similar to the one they'd been following for the past two hours. This, too, unravelled between the dove-grey and blue of the summer landscape.

"Well done," Hugh said before he could stop himself. He looked apologetically across, before adding with some firmness, "We stay on this for the best part of sixty kilometres."

Clare's fingers rested lightly on the steering wheel, her fine boned profile flecked by sun that pierced the poplars' cover and gave a luminous glow to her skin's faint down. Wind through the small car's open windows riffled the neat cap of her dark-brown hair.

"Message understood," she said, smiling, but keeping her eyes on the road.

Hugh folded the map and settled back into his seat, short-sleeved shirt clammy against his skin.

They'd been driving now for some three hours, with only one brief stop. Through the car's windows rushing air pressed warmly on his skin, and he had not slept well last night, their first in France. He closed his eyes and as he did so memories of the previous evening's humiliations re-awoke.

He saw again their arrival at the hotel into which Clare had booked them. A youth in black trousers and white shirt reeking of perspiration showed them to their room and, as he backed out, gazed in contemptuous disbelief at the banknote Hugh had offered him. "Sorry." Abashed, Hugh had taken it back, leaving Clare to hand over a euro note. But then, turning away, intending to swing his bag onto a chair, he knocked over a floor lamp, in the process breaking the lamp's expensive-looking shade. He'd had to pay for that, an exorbitant amount it seemed to him, but then what would you have? So he understood the ferocious-looking woman who handed him the bill to say when he settled up for their room and dinner.

Ah, yes, the dinner. A two hours' nightmare. The hovering waiter and the poker-straight sommelier at first refused to address any remark to Clare, whose French was excellent. Instead, they spoke exclusively to Hugh. "Oui" he said to whatever he was offered until Clare, laughing, said, "Hugh, are you sure you want *three* starters?" And Hugh, wiping sweaty palms on the napkin that had been settled round him, agreed that one would be sufficient.

"Why don't you order for both of us?" he suggested. A masterstroke, he thought, not having anticipated the degree to which his demotion was treated as proof positive of general incapacity.

From then on it was Clare who was asked whether she might like to taste the wine, Madame whose opinion was sought on how their beef was to be presented, Madame who was gravely consulted as to the cheeses they might prefer, and, at the end of the meal, the bill was laid beside Madame's coffee cup, accompanied by a smile in which admiration was overlaid by sincere condolences, the waiter murmuring to her in what seemed to be a rather too familiar manner. Clare smiled her reply.

"What did he say?" Hugh leant across to ask Clare as the man withdrew.

"He said that the bill could be presented in the morning, but as for service…"

"His tip?"

"Service is so much nicer." Clare pronounced it in the French way.

Hugh took out a 20 euro note and laid it on the table. "Is that nice enough?"

After this, it was unsurprising if regrettable that his performance in bed proved less accomplished than either of them hoped for; nor was his embarrassment lessened by Clare's "Oh, well, never mind," followed by the speed with which, having turned away from him, she seemingly fell into a deep sleep.

***

The car was slowing. Hugh opened his eyes in time to realise that Clare was expertly manoeuvring between Citroens parked anywhichway under a line of trees. Behind and to either side of the trees were town houses.

"Are we here?" he asked. "What time is it?"

"Time for a drink." Clare said, swivelling herself out of the driver's seat, her movements as always thrilling him by their youthful grace.

He levered his way up and out of the car and stood blinking in the afternoon sunlight. Clare was already making for a nearby *bar tabac*, careful to avoid a large black dog of uncertain pedigree which lay sprawled outside a darkened *boucherie*, its mouth agape to show yellow fangs and a strap-like tongue.

France was full of rabid dogs. As Hugh edged past, the dog raised its head and opened its eyes, all in one movement, and as it did so its tail rose and fell.

What was the French for "Good dog"?

But the dog's head fell back, its eyes closed, and sleep resumed its solitary reign.

In the bar's dim light Hugh made out a few men in overalls sitting at the zinc-topped tables before glasses of variously coloured liquids. They looked briefly and indifferently at the newcomers, then returned to their newspapers and talk.

"Tell you what," Hugh said to Clare, "why don't you order for us while I find a table?"

Clare looked briefly around at the unoccupied room. "I think I can spot one," she said.

Hugh made for a table as far away as possible from the bar and the threat of conversation. He'd decided to give up any pretence of understanding, let alone being able to speak, French. Weeks ago, when Clare had first suggested this holiday, he'd felt a stab of panic in his bowels. He should never have told her about his proposed study of Northern Gothic. But she, caught up by an enthusiasm with which he'd certainly meant to impress her, at once suggested this fortnight's tour for them both: Rouen, Chartres, Vézelay, (not Gothic, she agreed, but on no account to be missed), Rheims. He was trapped, could hardly back out or say he had other calls on his time—not when he'd just left his wife for her. And so here he was in France and thus far, he knew, not appearing to best advantage. Slumped in a hard wooden chair, he comforted himself with the thought that once he and Clare began to inspect the cathedrals his specialist knowledge would more than make up for present inadequacies. Then, as the saying went, he'd come into his own.

He looked up. Clare was walking toward him, closely followed by the barman who bore in his hands a round tray on which stood their drinks. The barman's eyes were fixed in shameless admiration on Clare's tight-jeaned bottom. Having arranged the drinks, the man pulled out a chair for Clare, glancing as he did so from her to Hugh and back again, a glance that none too subtly blended approval (of Clare) and disdain (for her companion), tucked the tray under his arm, and after a cursory bow retreated to the bar.

Clare's tall glass was, she explained, filled with fresh lime juice, further driving being required of her before they reached Rouen. His, smaller, held a colourless liquid that smelt of aniseed. "Pernod," Clare said, "you can drink boring old beer in England, but for the moment, cher ami, you're in France, and will do as the French do. Oh, sod. He's forgotten the water. You need water for that drink."

"It doesn't matter," Hugh said, "I can drink it neat."

"You most certainly *can't*. It is not permitted, monsieur." Clare was mock-insistent. "Drink pernod without water and it will rot more than your socks." She looked teasingly at him. "Well, off you go. Ask him for water. You know the French for *water*, surely?"

Without answering, Hugh got up and made his way to the bar. The barman, arms folded across his none too clean singlet, hands tucked comfortably under armpits, looked up from his newspaper as Hugh, standing in front of him, coughed.

"L'eau," Hugh said carefully.

The barman nodded. "'Ello, yourself," he said. Then he returned to reading his newspaper.

Hugh went back to Clare.

"I'm not getting anywhere with the barman," he said. "He doesn't understand French."

"Hugh," Clare said, "the barman *is* French."

"Well, he doesn't understand the French for water." Hugh sat down.

"Oh, for God's sake," Clare said, which was by no means the first time of late, Hugh thought, she had used that phrase.

She pushed her chair back, made briskly for the bar and almost immediately returned with a white-glazed jug on the side of which was printed Pastis 51.

"What did you try him on," Hugh asked, as he poured water into his glass and watched the liquid turn opalescent. "Urdu?"

***

But some weeks later, when they were back in England and installed in the flat Hugh had found for them, he enjoyed telling the story against himself. He told it to Allan and Joyce when they came round for dinner one evening in late September, though afterwards, as the couple were driving home, Joyce told her husband that she hadn't much liked Hugh's "little act."

"Act?" Allan asked, steering the car through gradually widening roads that led from city centre to outer suburbs. "What do you mean?"

"Oh, that show of being ever so 'umble. We were meant to lap up his story of being the dumbwit. 'Clare is *much* cleverer than me.' Hugh Montague, born-again feminist. Didn't you notice how he was looking at me all the time he wasn't pawing her, wanting my approval."

"He's in love," Allan said, as he swung the car up the steep slope to their house. "He's a happy man."

"*He* may be in love, I doubt that *she* is."

Allan brought the VW to a stop outside their garage. "She looked happy enough to me."

"Ah, but you don't know how to read the signs." Joyce unclipped her seat-belt, prepared to leave the car. "You ain't got no feminine intuition," she said, in passable imitation of Bronx. Then, in her own voice, "What's the betting she'll be off before long. Once the gloss is chipped away and under the appearance of Distinguished Intellectual she'll see him for what he is. Pure, unadulterated nerd."

"Unfair," Allan said, though laughing. "There are plenty of students who'll tell you that Hugh is one of the department's best lecturers. You're hard on him because you're Angela's friend."

They were in the house before Joyce spoke again. Then, as she took off her coat, she said, emphatically, "Angela is well rid of him."

Following her down the hall, Allan asked, "Is that what Angela thinks? What about the kids?"

"They'll be fine," Joyce said.

"Hmm."

In the kitchen now, Joyce turned to her husband and, without speaking, reached up a hand and stroked his grey hair.

"Ah, love, love," he said.

They looked into each other's eyes, held the look for some moments before Joyce spoke, this time her voice low. "Yes," she said. "Love."

***

"I thought that went pretty well," Hugh said, as he and Clare cleared away the detritus of the evening's meal. The onion soup he had prepared, followed by Clare's version of cassoulet which was washed down by Allan's gift of a Merlot and then followed by fruit and camembert, had provided the perfect setting for an over-the-table account of the fortnight Hugh and Clare had spent inspecting French cathedrals. It was a discussion that continued as the four of them left the table to sit, Allan and Joyce in easy chairs, and, side-by-side on a futon, Hugh and Clare, Hugh holding Clare's hand as he let his friend and head of department understand that he had been on a working holiday and that with Clare's essential help he had spent a good deal of time pondering whether it was Chartres or Rheims which could be held to embody the essential spirit of the Gothic.

"Gothic what?" Joyce asked.

"Gothic as noun, I think Hugh means," Allan said to his wife. "Not Gothic as adjective."

As in "The spirit of Gothic," Clare said.

"Oh, I see," Joyce said, responding to the young woman's quizzical—was it?—tone of voice. "I seem to remember that Forster called *that* spirit a denial of the flesh."

"Forster?" Hugh looked startled.

"E.M. Forster," Joyce said. "The novelist."

"Oh." Hugh was relieved. Not an authority he'd failed to consult. He pretended to consider the words. "Well, there's something in what he says. When you walk into one of those vast spaces you certainly understand how resistant the medieval imagination was to the spirit of secularism."

"Unquote," Allan said.

Hugh laughed, a small, self-conscious laugh. "Yes, I confess. A sentence from the work in progress."

"And is progress satisfactory?"

This time laughter was exchanged for a grave assent as Hugh, meeting the older man's gaze, said, "More than satisfactory." He leant to kiss Clare's cheek. "Thanks to my assistant," he said.

***

"Do you think he *will* write the book?" Joyce asked Allan, as they lay in bed, listening to an early autumn wind sifting through leaves of sycamore that lined the bottom of their garden.

"I certainly hope so," Allan said, "and this time I think he just might."

"Then you've got a good deal to answer for," Joyce said.

She rolled on her side and was soon asleep.

But Allan, lying awake, thought about her remark. It was he who had urged Hugh to write a book-length essay on the medieval imagination. Colleagues in the history department of the city's older university, Allan Whitehead and Hugh Montague had over the years developed a friendship which owed much to their shared sense of being in a den dominated by ageing and mangy lions; and though Allan's frequent, highly-praised publications, his emergence first as an historian of national and then of international importance, and his eventual appointment as professor and head of department led to an inevitable, if slight, distancing, especially as Hugh's few articles, which appeared in the mustier journals, produced little by way of academic advancement, the friendship survived.

It did so partly from genuine mutual respect, and partly because, as Hugh once carefully explained to Angela, "Allan's a high-flier, whereas I'm earth-tethered." The remark had the merit of making him feel serious about himself, a solid, feet-on-the-ground sort of person, one enhanced less by the succession of off-the-peg, two-piece suits he bought than by the warm regard in which he was held by students who valued the time he spent correcting their essays as well as lending an ear to their more personal problems. He was, as many of them said, "a decent bloke."

And then, one lunchtime, as he and Allan were downing a pint in the staff club, Allan mentioned that a "small academic publisher" would be visiting him for lunch the following day in the hope of sniffing out suitable contacts, and that the publisher, Kyle Lombard, would surely be interested in hearing from Hugh about his long-projected study of the medieval imagination. It might therefore be a good idea for Hugh to join the two of them for lunch. What Allan *didn't* say was that this was not only in Hugh's interest, it was by way of being an order. And he didn't say it because there was no need to do so. They both knew that book publication was becoming the only measure by which higher authority—that is, university administration—judged whether the moving finger should point at those whose publication record could be judged less than satisfactory, and that the finger would then point toward the Exit door. Publish or be gone.

So Hugh went to lunch with Allan and Kyle Lombard, and by the time the meal came to an end he had agreed to supply the latter with a 60,000 word monograph on northern gothic. "What I'm looking for," Lombard said, as he sipped Perrier water and contemplated without pleasure the heaped plate an assistant at the self-service counter had tentatively identified as steak-and-kidney pudding, "is a work that will combine accessibility with no sacrifice of scholarly..." he gazed about him....

"Integrity?" Hugh offered.

"Exactly," Lombard said. Fixing Hugh with an air of candid scepticism, he asked, as he leant across the table, "Now, for the all-important question. Do you think you can deliver to time?"

"Yes," Hugh said, adding, "absolutely." Absolutely was, he had noticed, the new way of saying yes. So he said it again, "Absolutely," and this time he put the stress on the third syllable and inhaled the publisher's mingled scents of aftershave and body lotion.

"Good. I'll have a contract drawn up as soon as I'm back in London."

Lombard stood. "Can't manage an advance, I'm afraid. The stuff of dreams, advances. But there'll be a proper royalty basis. Besides, I'm sure you're not in it for the money."

"Absolutely," Hugh said, then, watching Lombard use his paper napkin to flick some invisible crumbs from what had to be designer jeans, amended his remark to "Absolutely not."

But Lombard had turned to Allan. "Thanks for lunch," he said. "I don't suppose I can persuade you to offer us anything, though it goes without saying that we'd be honoured to have you on board."

Without speaking, Allan managed to communicate his regret.

"No, I thought not," Lombard said. "Well, you know where to find us."

He reached inside his woollen navy-blue jacket, removed a card from his leather wallet, and gave it to Hugh. "We'll be in touch," he said. "No, finish your coffees. I can find my own way out. Goodbye Mr. Montgomery."

"Montague, actually," Hugh said, "Dr. Montague."

But Lombard was already steering between tables, on his way to the door.

***

Two months later, having signed a contract with KL Publishing which committed him to producing a final typescript of his work within twenty-four months, Hugh had gained, so he explained to Angela, a new purpose to his professional and intellectual life.

"Which means we can expect to see even less of you."

Hugh, who was intending to spend the evening in his study, paused at the door of the drawing room where his wife sat, her down-turned mouth implying a bitterness he tried not to acknowledge.

"You see me every day." He wondered whether to attempt a disarming laugh. "The four of us eat together, we talk together…"

"*Talk*. *We* don't talk. *You* talk. The rest of us *listen*."

He knew all too well what would follow. The accusation, which of late had come with increased bitterness, that he thought his wife too thick to deserve more than a series of condescending put-downs, a way of speaking to her and the two children as though all three were on the same primeval level, that because she, Angela, hadn't been to college she couldn't possibly be expected to understand let alone sympathise with the workings of Hugh's mighty intellect, that *of course* as a trainee nurse he'd met at a student dance she was simply a bit of crumpet to be bedded and then forgotten, a forgetting which she wished had been possible and *would* have been possible if he'd used a bloody contraceptive, that if he thought she enjoyed being lectured to about the demands of the academic life he could think again, that in particular she had had it up to here with his nightly reports on the 'issues' which he alone, Saint Hugh Montague, could help students deal with, given that no other lecturer would either recognise them or be bothered to lend an ear to young people's grievances….

He closed the door before she could begin.

But his study was no longer a refuge from the woe that is in marriage. Angela's clamant unvoiced accusations sounded in his head. And when he turned away from his desk the first thing he noticed was the black leather jacket he had thrown over a chair when he got back from the university.

Oh, that jacket. He had bought it on impulse soon after the lunch meeting with the head of KL Publishing. It was in all senses, he considered, a radical break from his suits, though the first time he wore it Angela was provoked to especially derisive comment. Was he perhaps hoping to be mistaken for a TV pundit? Or some sort of a media type? Or was he simply happy to look a bloody poseur?

Ah, never mind his wife's barbs. He would wear the jacket to this year's Finalists' Party.

***

The party, an annual event which had begun existence before either Allan or Hugh joined the department, was always held on the evening degree results were announced. In years gone by it had been held in the department itself, but of late the venue was an upstairs room of a city pub, where, after a couple of hours' awkward conversations, the students headed off to a night club while faculty members went home.

Some lecturers brought their partners, though Hugh discouraged Angela from attending. "Afraid I'll say something stupid, no doubt," she said, when, after she'd once asked why she couldn't be with him, he explained that the occasion provided a last opportunity to talk with students who had been in his care for three years and who were now about to step into an uncertain future.

"And I'll be in the way while you gaze tenderly into their eyes and let them know how much you care for them. The women students, that is." Her laugh was not a friendly one. "I could do the same for the males."

He knew she didn't mean it, but couldn't prevent himself from saying, more tight-lipped than he'd intended, "I leave that sort of thing to Bletchley", Bletchley being a younger colleague whose un-anxious pursuit of campus wives and even students was widely rumoured to be not without its successes.

All the same Hugh found himself meeting the eye of a woman student he didn't recognise while a small group gathered round him in the City Arms, listening as he spoke about the book on which he was working. "But," he said, bringing his few remarks to an end, "no more reports from the coal face. We're here to enjoy and to celebrate your achievements." His words were the signal for the group to break up.

But she remained, looking, it seemed to him, uncertain, at a loss.

To help her, he said, "I'm sorry, I don't, I'm afraid, know your name."

The press of students, tangle of shouted comments, of glasses being raised, clinked, the hubbub of pub noise, forced her to step closer before she said, "Clare Stevens. I'm not in the History department. I came with my boy-friend."

And when he looked at her enquiringly, she named a youth whom Hugh knew well enough: a clever, supercilious student, who made a point of sitting in the back row of lectures, seemingly indifferent to Hugh's attempt to enthuse his audience about pre-Reformation Europe, though from time to time his face would relax into a smile that seemed nearer to a smirk.

Hugh glanced about him. "I don't see him," he said.

"That's because he isn't here." She lowered her gaze, then lifted her eyes to his as she said, "He used this evening to tell me it's over. As of now, I'm his ex-girlfriend."

"I'm sorry." An explosion of laughter from a group nearby caused him to shout the words.

"Don't be," she shouted back, and, as the noise subsided, she added more quietly, "He's a shit."

Yes, he is, Hugh thought, looking at the young woman standing close in front of him, not quite meeting her gaze as he took in her dark-brown hair, cut short to reveal the high forehead, arched eyebrows above luminous, dark eyes, her regular nose, the wide lips and rounded chin. Not beautiful, maybe, but undeniably attractive, her body outlined in the dark-red shirt which, open to reveal a thin, silver band at her throat, was tucked into a pair of black jeans.

Trying for small talk, anything to keep her attention, he asked, "What will you do now?" Then, seeing her confused look, added, "I didn't mean.... I mean, I assume you're a finalist, too...."

She nodded. "French. Yes, I got an upper second. Don't we all." A shrug, as though to dismiss the matter of degree status.

"I'll probably end up teaching though I'm in no hurry to decide. I'm going to hang on here for a week or two, then I think I'll give myself a holiday in France." A small laugh. "Now I'm on my own I can go wherever I like. And when I like." She finished her drink, which seemed to loosen her tongue. "I've enough money to tide me over for a few months. After that I suppose I'll have to find what my dad would call gainful employment."

He said, "Can I buy you another drink, or are you…" He looked round to see that the crowd was thinning out as students began drifting away, no doubt heading to the night club of choice. Faculty members had already shaken hands with various of their tutees, said their goodbyes and left.

"Yes. I'd like another drink," she said. "Vodka with ice."

And when he returned with the drink and she took it from him, she said, "I don't much fancy clubbing, not tonight."

He looked at her face, expecting to see signs of sorrow. But she smiled up at him, raised her glass. "Down with all shits," she said.

They clinked glasses and he said, motioning behind her, "We could sit down."

She turned to look at where he was gesturing, turned back to him, said, "Fine by me," and a moment later they were sitting facing each other across a table strewn with empty glasses.

***

And that was how it began. Before long Clare was dropping into his office for small talk, though she never arrived before he'd completed his morning's work; they'd drive somewhere in her car, an old, beat-up Fiesta, or, when the weather was good—as it mostly was—she might arrive with a thermos and sandwiches which they'd take to a nearby canal towpath. Hugh, free of his teaching commitments and with few administrative responsibilities, was steadily accumulating material for his work in progress. Clare, who seemed genuinely interested in what he told her about northern Gothic, was marking time. She was, she told him, thinking she might enrol for a TEFL course but that wouldn't start until the autumn and in the meantime she had nothing to do but relax and enjoy herself. The former boyfriend was never mentioned.

Nor did Hugh mention Angela and his children. He sometimes wondered whether Clare knew about his family, but decided that if so she didn't mind—and what after all *was* there to mind, theirs being a casual friendship, one based on the casual pleasures of talk, and a shared interest in medieval architecture.

Yet on days when she failed to come to the office he would arrive home, temper frayed by what he claimed was a setback in his research. "There's no need to take it out on the kids," Angela would protest when he shouted at them for some minor offence. "It would help if you thought less about your bloody work and more about us."

Hugh would be contrite. "Sorry, sorry. I *do* think about you."

"Not to the point of taking us on holiday."

He was all consideration. "I'm genuinely sorry about that. But I *must* get this book written. My—*our*—future depends on it." He stared with desperate earnestness at his wife, tried not to notice her pinched, bitter expression. "Six uninterrupted weeks of work is a godsend. And," he tried for cheerful reassurance, "you know you and the kids will enjoy being at Sarah's."

"Oh, no doubt about that," Angela said. "I'll have a wonderful time persuading them to eat the vegetarian pap my sister provides; and she'll have an equally wonderful time denying me access to alcohol and tobacco. In fact we'll have such an absolutely bloody wonderful time that I can't imagine how we'll be able to tear ourselves away and come back to this." And she gestured expansively about the kitchen where she and Hugh were washing up after the evening meal.

The following afternoon, when he and Clare were strolling along a canal towpath near the campus, Hugh let drop into their casual talk the confession that he was finding difficulty in summarising Aquinas's arguments for God's existence, and that this, he had come to feel, was linked to, and even caused by, his being under pressure from what he called "other quarters". He was at once ashamed of his words, but Clare gave no hint of understanding what he might be implying.

The afternoon was overcast and rain began to fall. "Damn," Hugh said, realising they were some distance from shelter. But Clare said "Yonder I spy salvation," pointing to a row of terraced houses on the opposite bank. "Ghetto City," she said, "aka student alley, where I have my room. Come on, we can shelter there," and she began to run toward the narrow packhorse bridge ahead of them.

***

Looking back, Hugh could never decide whether Clare had intended that the afternoon of rain should be the one when they became lovers. She couldn't, after all, have planned the rain. She could, though, have hoped for its arrival when she chose the canal walk. And he, he realised, had hoped for what resulted when, initially astounded though he was by the unabashed ardour of her love-making, he lost himself in her.

That, at least, was how he explained himself to Allan, when, a week later, having kissed Angela and his children goodbye as they set off for Stockport, he asked for an interview with his friend. Sitting in Allan's office, he explained as well as he could about his feelings for Clare, how he was now convinced that his future lay with her, that his marriage had, to coin a phrase, for long been reduced to the ashes of its former fire; and that he would of course make provision for Angela and the children, whom he was convinced would be better off without him. "She'll be far happier with me off the premises."

***

And that was what Allan had related to Joyce, who called Hugh a pathetic creep, words she now repeated to her husband as they lay, side by side, after their evening with Hugh and Clare, listening to the wind of autumn stirring the sycamore leaves. "He's a happy man," Allan said, sleepily.

***

And meanwhile, on the other side of the city, Hugh and Clare were arguing about what Clare insisted was Joyce Whitehead's disapproval of his relationship with someone his head of department's wife obviously saw as a bimbo or heartless marriage wrecker, an insistence from which Hugh couldn't budge her no matter how earnestly he explained that he and the Whiteheads were old friends and that although Joyce probably took Angela's part, at least for the moment, she would come round to understanding why matters were better as they now were.

Clare was silent for a few moments after that. Finally, she said, "Hugh, I'm sorry. I got you into this. I *did* make the running, I know, and I apologise."

"There's nothing to apologise for," he said. Solicitously, he added, "you go to bed, you have to be up early now you've started your course. I'll finish clearing away the dishes."

He was at the sink when he heard Clare enter the kitchen. She came up behind him, put a hand to his neck, said, her voice muffled, "Sorry," and went.

When he had finished washing up and stacking the crockery, he undressed and, carrying his clothes, tiptoed into the room where, he could tell from the breathing coming from the futon, Clare was already asleep. Easing himself under the duvet, he, too, composed himself for sleep.

***

He was woken by the repeated beep of his phone. It came from the kitchen, where he'd left it overnight.

"Hugh," Angela's voice. Distant, curt. "Why on earth haven't you answered the phone? This is the third time I've had to ring you."

"Sorry." Standing by the draining board, he looked at his watch. Half-past nine. "I was late last night," he said, trying to clear his head. "I was…. We were… we were entertaining. Sorry."

Difficult to tell whether the snort was one of disapproval or disbelief. "Well, never mind that. I need to remind you that you're to collect the children from school this afternoon. You're looking after them this weekend, remember. I've made up a bed for you in the spare room. And you are *not* to bring that woman here, do you understand?"

"No," he said, "of course not." Clare and he had already agreed that she would use the weekend to visit her parents, in Southampton. She had packed her bag before their guests arrived and it was, he saw at a glance, no longer where she'd put it the previous evening, beside their coats.

"In case of emergency," Angela said, "I've left an address and telephone number. In full view. On the dining table."

"You're going out of town?" He tried to recall whether she'd told him of her movements but couldn't. "Anywhere interesting?"

"You don't need to know," Angela's voice was briskly dismissive. "Nor who's coming with me." This time there was a smothered giggle.

"Oh?" But the phone had gone dead.

Had Angela found herself a man? Oddly piqued by that thought, Hugh felt the kettle, cold already, filled it, and, when he had made himself a cup of tea, took it over to the table and sat down.

"Sorry." It occurred to him now that the word he had used to excuse himself to Angela was Clare's last word to him before she disappeared to bed. He had been asleep when she left for college at least two hours ago, taking her weekend bag with her. He must wash, dress, and put in a morning's work on campus, his last chance of uninterrupted study before the students returned.

And after lunch he would have to shop for the kids' supper. Had he enough money or must he pay a visit to his bank? Better consult his wallet. He reached behind him for his leather jacket, draped over the back of his chair, and as he did so felt the scrape of paper against his wrist. A note had been pinned to the jacket's lining.

His stomach lurched. Even before he read it he knew what it would say. And it did.

A is for....

Walking through the back streets of Aegina's port town one summer afternoon in 2015, I came on a second-hand shop I'd not noticed before. I like such places, such curiosity shops. You can spend half an hour rummaging through the contents and, among the usual tat, you invariably unearth something that takes your fancy, buy it and go on your way. Another bargain, you assure yourself, choosing not to hear the voice telling you that what you have in hand or pocket is yet another victory for momentary desire over better judgement. One more object to add to the clutter which, over the years, is threatening to turn your home into its own curiosity shop.

 This shop, though, seemed without promise. It held nothing but tat. Tat, tat, and more tat. Assortments of rusting kitchenware, tied with string, were heaped on top of cupboards from which paint was peeling and whose doors wouldn't close, typewriters without ribbons, their half-raised keys locked into metal claws, were rammed against superannuated radios, a TV, its screen stove in, balanced uncertainly on the blades of a rusted lawnmower; old tables and chairs, some straight-backed, others leaking their innards, covered much of the floor space.

 As for the walls, they were hung with fly-spotted mirrors in mahogany frames, blurry black-and-white photographs from the earlier part of the twentieth-century showing Aegina's caique-filled harbour, family portraits, men with huge moustaches and women wrapped in shawls, around them assortments of over-dressed children. Least interesting of all were the amateur paintings of pistachio orchards, olive groves, and, inevitably, the island's temple, its ruined splendour made ridiculous by inept draughtsmanship, faulty perspective, and colours that never were on sea or land.

I was about to leave when I spotted beneath one of the sagging chairs a paperback book, pushed almost out of sight, as if someone had made an ineffectual effort to hide it, as if even in this fusty shop it's presence was an embarrassment. I bent, hoicked the book out and, in the shop's gloomy light, peered at the battered cover. A bronze mask that looked as though it came from ancient Greece peered back at me. Above it was the book's title. *The Mask of Demetrios*. A study of pre-Hellenic culture, perhaps? But no. I recognised the author's name. Eric Ambler.

"How much?" I asked the shop-keeper, a young Pakistani who sat behind a desk smoking as he punched numbers into his cell-phone. He looked up, shrugged, leaving it to me to make an offer.

"Two euros?"

He nodded.

Later, sitting on the balcony of our rented flat above the small harbour at Faros—the word means lighthouse and, this being Greece, there is no lighthouse—a glass of local retsina at my elbow, I opened Ambler's book. I had never previously read any of his novels though I knew he was much admired by aficionados of that branch of crime fiction usually called "Thrillers." Among these admirers were several poet friends of mine, all of whom assured me that Ambler wasn't any old thriller writer. He wasn't a guilty pleasure to be pursued in secret. He wasn't *sub rosa*, wasn't "under the chair."

Far from it, in fact. Once back in England I discovered that Ambler has become academically respectable. In his *Cambridge Guide to Literature in English*, Dominic Head notes that Ambler's books "are all sustained by a successful formula, usually involving an ordinary Englishman who becomes caught up in a web of international espionage and intrigue." And David Glover, in a vast compilation on *Twentieth-Century English Literature* remarks that for Ambler, "the thriller revolves around decency under pressure.... And, as often as not, it is market capitalism, in the shape of an amoral corporation or trust, that is the ultimate villain." So that's alright.

Having read what Head and Glover had to say, it occurred to me to look again into a book I'd had on my shelves for years, Paul Fussell's *Abroad: British Literary Travelling Between the Wars.* Fussell, it turned out, has nothing to say about Ambler. He does, though, quote a telling remark of Graham Greene's. "We were a generation brought up on adventure stories who had missed the enormous disillusionment of the First War," Greene says, "so we went looking for adventure." And Greene was a champion of Ambler's work.

The Mask of Demetrios, has adventures aplenty. Its central character, Charles Latimer, is an Englishman "who for fifteen years had lectured in economics at a minor university." In pursuit of research for a book, Latimer is travelling by train across Europe when, through no fault of his own, he finds himself involved with a number of dodgy and dangerous characters. They all seem to be travelling under false names and/or identities, their nationalities and the nature of their business in continual doubt, and as a result of his involvement with these dubious figures Latimer spends time in various foreign cities where he becomes witness to murder and mayhem. Ambler's novel is, you might say, hokum, high-class hokum, well-written and ingeniously plotted, but hokum nevertheless.

But this would be to slight its atmosphere of menace. Ambler wasn't of course alone in adopting as *mise en scène* a train thundering through foreign countries so as to create this atmosphere. All those night-time stops at places with unpronounceable names, all those long corridors down which shadowy figures are hurrying or vanishing into locked compartments, all those languages you can't understand and in which, for all you know, men are planning your death. Besides, there is a quality of recklessness about the iron monster's speed which brings with it the threat of collision, of—forgive me—going off the rails. Think of Edward Upward's *The Railway Accident* and, far less known, but in most ways superior, the first half of Arnold Bennett's 1927 novel, *Accident.* Think of Greene's *Stamboul Train* of 1932, and, two years later and most famously, Agatha Christie's *Murder on the Orient Express.*

Even so, *The Mask of Demetrios* has a distinctive quality to it, difficult to pin down, but, once encountered, unmistakeable. The air of sinister unease it exudes isn't confined to Ambler's handling of his disreputable characters, effective though that is. It is more diffusive: it is the bacillus infecting the narrative. Characters who offer friendship are almost certainly not to be trusted. Cities where you think you know how to find your way may lead you up blind alleys or into quarters where you realise you have lost your bearings. It's safer to get back on the train.

But is it? Can you be sure the train is going in the right direction, or did the railway porter who silently helped you aboard deceive you about its eventual destination? If so, why? And now that the train has begun to move out into a dark landscape can you trust the guard who comes to scrutinize first your ticket, then you, then backs out of the compartment having exchanged a smile with the other, male, occupant who entered the compartment immediately after the train left the station and is now sitting opposite you but will not speak and does not meet your eye; and why, later, do the customs officials who study your papers stare at you with—contempt, is it? Indifference? What do they know that you don't?

Only when I had finished my reading of Ambler's novel did I look for the date of publication. 1939. Ah.

***

I was born in 1937. A year later my father lost his work as an insurance salesman in Exeter, and while he went from town to town in search of new employment, my mother and two small children—my sister, was born in late 1938—returned to live at her parents' house in Wimbledon. After some months of pounding the streets, as the phrase goes, my father was taken on by the Cross Keys Insurance Company to be a door-to-door salesman in the Coventry area. I have no idea how he came by the job. Perhaps through the good offices of one of his mother-in-law's several brothers, a plumber in the city who, as I found years later when my mother took my sister and me to visit him, lived near Coventry City's football ground, owned a motorbike and sidecar, his garage doubling as store-room for his trade's impedimenta, among which I recall racks of lavatory pans, wash-basins, gleaming taps, and lengths of copper pipe. He must have had business contacts across the city.

At all events, thanks to the Cross Keys Company, the family was now re-united. At the beginning of August, 1939, we moved into a small town house whose rent my father could afford. The house was, my mother later admitted, a poorly-built two up and downer, but at least we were together. Then, a month after our move, on 3 September, Chamberlain announced that the United Kingdom and France were at war with Germany. My father at once volunteered for active service and early in 1940, while he awaited his call-up papers, the Company transferred him to Leicestershire. It meant a further move, this time to a village close to Hinckley, where he rented another small, semi-detached house. Soon afterwards he was told he had been recruited into the Tank regiment. He left for training at Barnard Castle.

I retain fragments of memory from those times. One, which must belong to the Coventry period, is of sitting with my father at the front of the top deck of a double-decker bus and watching with appalled fascination as a train steams toward us through fields to our right. I am certain the train will crash into the bus but at the last possible moment it vanishes and we continue on our way unharmed. We had gone over a bridge, though only later was I able to make sense of the train's miraculous disappearance.

The other memory is unplaceable. I am walking at my mother's side as she propels a push-chair, or is it a pram, into which my sister is strapped. We are on a grassy path and to our right I notice rolls of what, years afterward, I realise must have been barbed wire.

"You mustn't go near that," my mother says.

"Why not?"

"Because it will hurt you." Does she also say, or is this a later invention of mine, "It's there to keep us safe from harm."

Two moments, two memories, that between them encrypt the anxiousness deep within my psyche.

***

"We went looking for adventure." Who are "we"? Not my parents for sure, nor for thousands upon thousands like them, who belonged to the lower-middle class, for whom money was always in short supply, and who grew up at a time when finding work was difficult and holding on to it even more so. Adventure was the last thing such people wanted. They aspired to nothing more remarkable than marriage, children, a roof over their heads, regular meals, and just enough money in their pockets to pay for modest forms of entertainment: an occasional visit to the theatre or cinema, an equally occasional Saturday evening dance at a local dance hall (not pub, pubs were not respectable), and the annual—and usually unpaid—week of summer holiday. None of these desiderata could be achieved without a regular income. Getting and spending we lay waste our powers. Perhaps, but for people like my parents most of what they got had to be spent on the bare necessities. And if you couldn't find work or the work you had was taken away, what then? The daily worries about putting food on the table, about being decently clothed, about paying the bills, the fear of what little you had being suddenly removed, was for many people the norm. It was the life they knew. The life they lived. Anxiety was their all-the-year-round weather.

My father, born in 1913, a younger son, left school with few if any formal qualifications. His own father, who had been wounded at Gallipoli, built up during the 1920s a business selling cutlery to hotels in the Torquay area. It filled the larder, clothed his wife and two sons, and eventually enabled him to buy a decent-sized house; but, even after he had enough money in the bank to purchase a small car, the "business", as his wife, my sternly forbidding paternal grandmother, insisted on calling it, was never more than a one-man operation.

Had his mother been less of a stickler for social propriety, my father, a promising footballer who at the age of 16 played a game or two for Exeter City, might have found work as a professional sportsman. But this was ruled out. It would have brought disgrace on the family. Only working-class youths could be professional footballers. That occupation, like so many others, was "common." My father therefore became a door-to-door salesman. That way, he got to wear a suit, together with collar and tie. He was respectable.

As for my mother, born in 1910, six years later than Greene (1904–1991), and a year younger than Ambler (1909–98), whom she outlived by five years, I'm certain that she habitually thought the world a dangerous place. All her life she remembered hearing from her bedroom the cries and yells of Armistice Day, November, 1918, and her parents' sudden show of exultance, which she interpreted as a profound relief. Not so much joy, more a lifting of dread. The killing had stopped. Young men would no longer be turned to dung.

By the time war came to an end her father was headmaster of an elementary school in South London. He had been spared war service less by his profession than because of his age—he was born in 1880 and when in 1916 the Derby Act came into force he was (just) over the age of conscription.

But he had other causes for concern. Training to become a teacher had lifted him out of the working class into which he was born—his father was a "family" butcher—but the pay was poor, although following the advice of H.A.L.Fisher, Oxford historian and President of Lloyd George's Board of Education in the days immediately after the war, the government raised the salaries of elementary school teachers. Fisher's argument was simple. The only way to improve the standard of those entering a profession dominated by aspiring working-class men and women was to make it attractive to a better class of student teacher.

In *Our Mutual Friend*, the snob gentleman, Eugene Wrayburn, taunts the schoolmaster, Bradley Headstone, whose name he can't be bothered to learn because "I can say Schoolmaster, which is a most respectable title." True respectability, Wrayburn means, belongs only to a gentleman, which Headstone will never be.

I never knew my maternal grandfather, who died at the beginning of 1940, not long after he and the school of which he was then in charge had been evacuated to Princes Risborough. To try to compensate for this ignorance, I decided to write a book about him for which I undertook considerable research. *The Good That We Do* reveals, I hope without sentimentality or special pleading, that H.W.S. Kelly was a good man, one who worked selflessly to educate generations of underprivileged London children. But I don't doubt that he was a stickler when it came to the social proprieties, and though my mother loved him I suspect that he could come the martinet.

It was all a matter of being respectable. Horace, "Hod", Kelly rose into a class—lower-middle—at a time when dress-code, manners, mode of speech, social decorum had all to be acquired and then unwaveringly obeyed. He knew his place, or thought he did, and he expected others to know theirs. I remember his widow, who during the war years lived with us, remarking with complacent approval that the wife of the local farmer who supplied our daily milk ration—she brought it in a large pail and used a scoop to fill our jug—always came to the back door. A farmer's wife was "Trade". Only ladies made so bold as to come to the front door. And yet before her marriage, my grandmother, whose own father was a successful tradesman—he owned a thriving ironmonger's store in Kenilworth—had worked in a milliner's shop. No doubt my grandfather made her aware that with marriage she had gained new status. Like Bradley Headstone, he was almost neurotically anxious to be thought respectable, and he passed this anxiety on to his only child.

It is easy to mock this. And in truth such endless deference to entirely arbitrary ways of behaving remains the curse of Englishness. We are the most class-conscious nation on earth, and it isn't good for us. But with my mother's fear of being caught out in one damned solecism or another went a kind of courage I have never needed to possess. I've always loved Marianne Moore's poem "Nevertheless" and especially its ending:

> The weak overcomes its
> menace, the strong over-
> comes itself. What is there
>
> like fortitude! What sap
> went through that little thread
> to make the cherry red!

Like so many of her class, my mother had fortitude. She learnt it from her father, she shared it with her husband. It is one of the four cardinal virtues. And though I doubt she could have listed them, the others, prudence, justice, and temperance, were also deeply ingrained in her consciousness. None, I think, is integral to a sense of adventure.

***

She was an avid reader. Among the authors and titles in the filled bookcase that always stood beside her easy chair I remember *Tell England* by Ernest Raymond, Warwick Deeping's *Sorrel and Son* (a favourite), Winifred Holtby's *South Riding*, books by Rafael Sabatini, Naomi Jacob, several novels by J.B. Priestley, the Daily Express *Illustrated History of the Great War*, two of Edward Marsh's anthologies of *Georgian Poetry*, besides Thomas Moult's *Best Poems of 1927*, and Ripley's *Believe It Or Not*. This last was a fat compendium of "impossible" phenomena like the cat with five heads, which, as with most of the other entries, turned out to have been inventions of the author, an American journalist.

Was Eric Ambler on the shelves? If so, I don't remember. But she enjoyed thrillers and crime fiction. Agatha Christie, Marjorie Allingham and Ngaio Marsh were all there, as were Edgar Wallace and John Buchan, whose *The Thirty-Nine Steps* she often re-read. She may well have borrowed works by Ambler from the library at Hinckley. If she did, I wonder what she made of them? At the very least, they would have confirmed her unstated belief that abroad was a dangerous place, that adventure was all very well but being at home was better. There, you feel safe.

This belief, this feeling, was the more desperately held because safety wasn't and couldn't be assured. Fortitude—resolute endurance—was essential in the face of threats, which, so experience taught, lurked all about. You had to endure possible slights from people who considered themselves a cut above you; you had to be always "presentable" and ensure that in addition to being fed and clothed your children must be taught their manners; you needed to keep an unremitting watch on expenditure. I can't believe an insurance salesman was well paid, but like other married women of her class my mother wouldn't have been allowed to find outside work to supplement her husband's meagre income. He was, after all, expected to keep her in the manner to which she was supposedly accustomed. She, meanwhile, once her father had given his permission for her marriage, was expected to fill her days in maintaining her new house—in her case a small, rented bungalow. There were daily routines. Monday—washday, Tuesday—cleaning the silver and furniture, Wednesday—bottling fruit and vegetables, Thursday—dress-making, knitting, darning and mending, Friday—shopping and baking of pies, cakes, biscuits.

Well, some of this, though by no means all, is guesswork. My mother was an intelligent woman who never thought her intelligence was of importance in her life. What counted was being safely married and obeying the rituals of marriage, and what therefore she feared most was the threat that her husband might at any time lose his work. That would have brought everything tumbling down. As for a while it did.

And then, at the beginning of September, 1939, came an even greater fear. The announcement of war brought with it the probability of a German invasion as well as the certainty of imminent bombing raids. The population was issued with gas-masks. Anderson shelters were dug at the bottom of gardens for those who could afford them. Those who couldn't were given Morrison steel tables to be erected in your dining room and under which you were to crawl whenever the warning siren of approaching enemy aircraft sounded its weird, eldritch howl. Death could at any time fall from the air, it might well arrive from the sea. Overcoming the dread, or at the least facing it, was, I want to say, for my mother and so many like her, a full-time occupation. And going with that must have been the sense of powerlessness in a world on fire, one heart-rendingly imaged at the end of Elizabeth Bishop's "Armadillo": *"O falling fire and piercing cry/ and panic, and a weak mailed fist/ clenched ignorant against the sky!"*

***

"We went looking for adventure." But that wouldn't have been why my father joined up. Nor can I imagine that a search for adventure prompted most of those who in 1939 volunteered for active service. They weren't gung-ho for battle. Some of those who volunteered loathed Fascism. They'd already met and fought against it at home—on London's Cable Street, for instance. Others had journeyed to Spain. But I suspect that most of the men and women who chose to join the armed services in September, 1939, did so from a sense of duty. It's a commonplace of history to say that an innocent desire for glory drove thousands to volunteer in August, 1914, but it's equally a commonplace to observe that by 1918 war weariness, disillusionment, even despair were widespread. The cries that reached my mother's ears on Armistice Day undoubtedly contained elements of jubilation; but they must have been accompanied by, subsumed under, shouts of relief. That was certainly what she thought she was hearing. At last the killing was over.

And then, a little over twenty years later, it began all over again. Who could possibly want that? Very few, I'd guess. But those who did, while not perhaps rejoicing in war, saw it as providing the chance for boy's-own heroism. These were the ones who, as Graham Greene's remark implies, thought of themselves as having missed out on the Great War. They included youths who, having joined flying clubs in the previous two decades, now became a kind of cavalry of the air, jousting among the clouds in one-to-one combat. (Fighter Command was always more glamorous than Bomber Command.) It isn't, however, their stories that engage me here. It's a rather different episode, one that encapsulates a number of contradictory elements I think of as redolent of the war: high-jinks and low dealing; fear and exultation; the insouciance of upper-class habits and the desperate, anxious lives of the poor.

***

It was called "Operation Mincemeat," and the title alone tells you a good deal about those who devised it. "I'll make mincemeat of you." It's a schoolboy boast, a blood-and-thunder threat. I won't simply beat you, I'll break you into little bits. "Utterly demolish", Brewer says in his *Dictionary of Phrase and Fable*. The *Oxford Dictionary of Idioms*, however, offers the more lenitive, "defeat easily in a fight, contest, or argument." This is more accurate. The boast has an element of derring-do but it also delights in exaggeration.

I don't suppose many households nowadays have a meat-mincer, though from time to time you might come across one in the kind of second-hand shop where I unearthed my dilapidated copy of *The Mask of Demetrios*. But they were once a standard kitchen item. A metal fixture about a foot high was bolted to the side of a table, at its base a thick screw-thread under a cup-shaped opening into which cold meat was forced, then ground down by the action of a handle which, as it turned, activated the screw-thread and caused obscene, pinkish-grey worms of meat to be extruded from a gargoyle mouth on the side of the mincer. I'll make mincemeat of you. The threat carries a frisson of disgust.

As for Operation Mincemeat itself, so unlikely, so fantastic, the odds against it stacked so high as to make its eventual success almost incredible, a bare-bones re-telling is all that's needed. Anyone wanting more should consult Ben MacIntyre's excellent *Operation Mincemeat* (2010), the forgiveable hyperbole of whose sub-title, "The True Spy Story that Changed the Course of World War II", hints at the sheer improbability of it all.

The story begins in 1943, with the allies poised to advance into mainland Europe, from which they had been exiled after the Dunkirk disaster. France, where the Germans remained in command and with the coast well fortified, was still beyond reach. Southern Europe was, however, a different matter. Spain might be neutral and so out of the question, but although Italy and Greece were in enemy hands both were potential targets for Montgomery's Eighth Army. Having dislodged Rommel from Egypt, this army was now ready to cross the Mediterranean and begin the long march up Europe through the Balkan States, from there into Austria, and then, finally, heartland Germany.

But which site to select for the first landings? Sicily was the obvious choice. Once secure that and the crossing to mainland Italy would be a cinch. There was, though, a problem. Mussolini might be a cardboard villain, and indeed by the middle of the year he was gone, but as he went down to defeat, German troops arrived in large numbers to strengthen Italy's defences. Besides, the Mediterranean was a dangerous sea to cross. U-boats could do colossal damage to transport ships, and the longer the journey the greater the chance of naval losses.

Greece, then? The Greeks had at first been under Italian control but now an altogether more brutal and efficient German occupying army ran the country. The Germans had control of Piraeus, Athens's port. But perhaps a landing might be attempted further north on the Greek mainland?

Which was it to be? Sicily or Greece?

A quick look at any map of the Mediterranean shows that Sicily is much nearer the coast of North Africa. A shorter crossing, a quicker landing, one that might be able to maintain the element of surprise. On the other hand, a landing in Greece, though it would take longer to get there, would have the advantage of bypassing Italy altogether, and from Greece you could fight your way through Yugoslavia, then onward to Berlin. This had obvious advantages, chief among them the well-organized Yugoslavian Resistance. Some of these were mountain fighters who had been part-trained by British forces on Malta; they were desperately keen to return to their home country and then set about the German occupiers.

But for all the attractions of this route, and for reasons it isn't necessary to go into here—there are plenty of books on the subject—the Allied High Command decided to make Sicily the starting point for their invasion from the south. The German High Command obviously suspected this would be their choice. But the Germans also knew that northern Greece, specifically Thessaloniki, remained a possibility. Could they be tricked into believing that *in fact* the Allies had decided to choose a spot in Greece as the place from which their planned invasion would begin? If so, that would greatly increase the chances of a successful Sicilian landing. It was this which prompted the grand hoax known as "Operation Mincemeat".

"Hoax"—"deceive by way of a joke" according to the O.E.D—seems at first blush an inadequate word to describe a plan on whose success the fate of the war might depend. But for those who were in on the plan, it was integral to the scheme they devised. A corpse was to be found floating off the Spanish coast. This corpse would apparently be from a plane that had crashed into the sea, and the dead man, dressed in the uniform of a naval officer, would have, chained to his wrist, an attaché case containing secret documents intended for High Command in

North Africa and detailing how an invasion of Greece was to be mounted.

In the course of *Operation Mincemeat*, Ben MacIntyre reports that those in any way involved in the operation who were still alive when he began his research, and who were willing to be interviewed, were unanimous in their opinion of the "corkscrew" minds of those who came up with the hoax. They were, one woman told MacIntyre, "able to see round corners." They were also, and perhaps unsurprisingly, oddities, eccentrics, misfits. One was an airman who never flew, another a seaman who never went to sea. But between them they fashioned a scheme which must, even to them, have seemed only too likely to come to grief at various points. So much so, that the chances of Operation Mincemeat actually succeeding were, they told MacIntyre—well, *composed* the stuff out of which adventure stories are made.

In the first place the planners had to find a suitable corpse. There was no difficulty in locating supplies of dead bodies at a time when air raids caused thousands of deaths among the civilian population, but the planners were after a particular kind of corpse. It had to be male, relatively young, undamaged; and then, as soon as one had been identified, the planners needed to get official permission to take it from a mortuary, which meant getting a coroner to agree to its removal into their keeping.

While the search for a corpse began, the planners were inventing a false identity for the dead "officer". His name was to be "Bill Martin", he had been to public school, then university, and he was even given a love life. Proof of this was a fiancée who went by the Betjeman-like name of "Pam"—one of the office girls in the War Office supplied a photograph of herself; and the receipt for an engagement ring costing £53 (about £15,000 in present day terms), bought from an "exclusive" jewellery firm, was pushed into Martin's wallet, together with "Pam's" photograph and several love letters from her, all of them written by the girl who had supplied the photograph. For good measure, the wallet also contained a letter from Martin's bank manager, complaining about the size of his overdraft.

"Bill Martin" now had an identity. And then a body became available. It was located among many stored at the St Pancras mortuary, and with the permission of the local coroner it was released into the custody of the planners who dressed it in officer's uniform and added the wallet and attaché case. That was easy. Footwear, however, proved a problem. The chosen corpse having been in the mortuary for some time, it proved impossible to fit boots onto its frozen feet. There was therefore an inevitable if frustrating delay of some hours while the corpse's feet were thawed out in front of a two-bar electric fire. But finally all was ready. Dressed and shod, the body was loaded into a van to be driven from London to the west coast of Scotland. There, it was to be transferred to a waiting submarine which would take it to coastal waters off Spain. "Bill Martin" would then be pushed into the sea and, with luck, spotted and brought ashore.

But now the planners hit a further snag. The van driver was a one-time motor-racing ace, presumably chosen for the task because he could drive fast through the night, all the way from London to Scotland, where he could be guaranteed to arrive in good time for the body to be transferred to the submarine. Unfortunately nobody had told the planners that the chosen driver suffered from restricted vision. As a matter of professional pride, however, he refused to wear glasses and as a consequence on several occasions nearly crashed the van on its journey north. At one point, he even drove straight over a roundabout.

Miraculously, the van arrived at its destination in time for the corpse to be got on board, and early one morning, some days later, and against all reasonable odds, "Bill Martin" was found by a fisherman, floating off the Spanish coast.

But why choose Spain for the site of the supposed aeroplane crash and "Bill Martin's" death? The answer is that this was all part of seeing round corners. Spain might be neutral but the planners knew that the British and Germans kept consular officials there, and while not exactly swarming with foreign spies, the country had more than its share of enemy agents, including Germans. Once the supposedly drowned officer's body was brought ashore it was examined by two local doctors plus the British Consul who had been summoned because the corpse was British. The Consul, who was in the know, was all-too aware that, despite the body being in a state of decomposition following its immersion in water and, then, exposure to the sun during its journey back to shore, the two medical men would soon realise that "Bill Martin" had been a corpse for a good deal longer than the presumed time of his death. Why not simply report that "Martin's" death was by drowning, the Consul asked the doctors, and release the body for burial.

Fortunately, his anxiety persuaded two German spies, who were also in on the autopsy, that the Consul had something to hide. Not so much the authenticity of the body as the nature of the papers in the attaché case chained to his wrist. Suspicion hardened into certainty when they were denied the chance to inspect the papers. By some ingenuity they nevertheless managed to get a peek at them. And what they saw was sufficient to send them hot-footing from the place. Shortly afterward, Berlin was assured that the planned Allied invasion would begin with an attempted landing on the Greek coast. Hitler took the bait. Arms, men, ships and planes were all diverted from Italy to Greece.

Against ridiculous odds, Operation Mincemeat succeeded. The Sicilian landings were managed with far fewer casualties than had originally been allowed for. Official estimates were for up to 30,000 troop deaths in the first week of invasion. In the event only 1400 were killed. The same estimates reckoned on as many as 300 ships being lost. A mere 14 were sunk or wrecked. The corkscrew minds that conceived the Operation and then worked out the details of how it should be conducted were vindicated.

***

"We went looking for adventure." Who were they, these men, and women, who could see round corners and who between them constructed an operation far more ingenious than Eric Ambler would have permitted himself. Unlike Patrick Leigh Fermor, the most outrageous example of such adventurers, whose capture of a German general on Crete led to his being heroised even by islanders who suffered brutal Nazi reprisals because of his madcap scheme, the people responsible for Operation Mincemeat were vicarious adventurers, for the most part stay-at-homers whose plans for action were put into operation by others. But at least they saved lives rather than costing them.

Anyone wanting to find more about them will be well advised to read MacIntyre's fine account. They will find there a gallimaufry of men and women whom the war threw together, some raffish, most well-connected, a few of them wealthy or in the kind of professions where money and status were easily come by. In short, the plotters represented the kind of people Greene would have had in mind when he wrote of those who, born too late for WWI, were hoping to atone for the accident of their birth dates. Even the St. Pancras coroner, Bentley Purchase, had the kind of old-school *sang-froid* that seems appropriate to both moment and occasion. At one point he even suggested to Ivor Montagu, one of those most closely involved in the plot, that at a pinch he, Montagu, might like to arrange to have himself run over by a bus, after which he could arrive at the mortuary in a hearse and Purchase would vouch for his availability as the corpse in the case.

Instead, Purchase cleared the way for a very different corpse to become "Bill Martin". And here the story narrows, deepens, and acquires a bitterly ironic flavour. MacIntyre provides an admirably full account of the man whose sad death made him available to become a kind of posthumous hero. What follows is a bare outline of the real "Bill Martin".

An illegitimate child, Glyndwr Michael was born on the fourth of January, 1909, in the Welsh mining village of Aberbargoed, where his father, Thomas Michael, worked as a colliery hauler. Thomas Michael and Glyndwr's mother were unmarried, because in 1888 the then twenty-year old Sarah Ann Chadwick had married another man, George Cottrell, by whom she had two daughters before she left him for Thomas. Glyndwr was born into a life of what seems to have been absolute poverty and squalor. His mother was illiterate—she had signed her marriage certificate with a cross—his father was syphilitic. (MacIntyre speculates that their son may have been born with congenital syphilis). The boy was part of a family which endlessly shifted from village to village in search of employment, never able to pay the rent on a succession of "dingy" houses (the word is Macintyre's), until in 1924, Thomas, by now in physical decline, stabbed himself in the throat. He survived, but died the following year of bronchial pneumonia. Fifteen years later, at the beginning of 1940, Glyndwr's mother had a heart attack and an aortic aneurism. "On 16 January, Glyndwr witnessed his mother's death certificate, buried her alongside his father in the Trealaw cemetery, and disappeared."

He probably headed for London in a desperate and, it seems, hopeless attempt to find work, because when, on 26 January, he was taken to St Pancras Hospital, it was from an abandoned warehouse where he had been found, "suffering from acute chemical poisoning." Glyndwr Michael was homeless, penniless, and almost certainly he had inadvertently poisoned himself by eating stale bread laced with rat poison. The autopsy suggested that he had probably swallowed little of the poison, but in his emaciated state what he ingested was sufficient to impair the liver function of a man the coroner described as "lunatic", and therefore likely to be a suicide case. In other words, Glyndwr was held to have killed himself "while the balance of his mind was disturbed." So that was that. In MacIntyre's bleak words, "A single man, illegitimate and probably illiterate, without money, friends, or family... had died unloved and unlamented."

But with his death those planning Operation Mincemeat had their corpse. A few months later, the body of "Bill Martin", the supposed victim of a crashed aeroplane, was discovered floating in the sea off Spain.

***

Everything about this story is threaded through with tragic irony. The "corkscrew minds" of those who, from privileged backgrounds, constructed an identity for "Bill Martin", is about as far as can be from the actual life of Glyndwr Michael. Nothing illustrates this more starkly, almost, I want to say, with greater irony, than the underwear in which the corpse was kitted out. MacIntyre notes that because of coupon rationing—the government's method of controlling in wartime what people could buy, including clothing— underwear of any kind was hard to come by. Michael's would no doubt have been in a shocking state, always supposing he had any at all. But Martin, so his creators had decided, was a product of public school and university, and from a moneyed background. His corpse therefore needed to be found in good quality underwear. How to come by vest and underpants that would pass muster? The problem was solved when H.A.L.Fisher was run over and killed "after attending a tribunal examining the appeals of conscientious objectors, of which he was chairman."

Though MacIntyre doesn't labour the irony, he does note that Fisher, an Oxford historian, was considered by his contemporaries to be "long-winded and pompous." No doubt, but, to repeat a point made earlier in this narrative, he was also the man who made it possible for my grandfather to earn a decent, though by no means generous, living; besides, as President of the Board of Education in Lloyd George's cabinet, Fisher furthered the cause of education for the underprivileged. This may not have helped the probably illiterate Glyndwr Michael, but Fisher's silk underpants helped convince those examining the body that it was the corpse of a bona fide, well-educated British Naval Officer who had on his person crucial instructions for the Allied invasion of mainland Europe.

MacIntyre ends his splendid book by noting that "Martin" was buried in Huelva's cemetery, where the inscription on his gravestone reads:

> William Martin
> Born 29th March 1907
> Died 24th April 1943
> Beloved Son of John
> Glyndwyr Martin
> And the late Antonia Martin of
> Cardiff, Wales
>
> Dulce Et Decorum Est Pro Patria Mori
>
> R.I.P

I imagine a shaft of glee that went through those responsible for the grand hoax as the gravestone was put in place. Their adventure was, in most senses of the word, accomplished.

Nor can it be said to have been compromised when, in 1997, the British government added the following to the gravestone in Huelva:

> Glyndwr Michael
> Served as Major
> William Martin, RN

If anything, this postscript merely intensifies the accomplishment. A legendary hero had been created out of base material. And very probably those involved would have been aware of a final irony. Glyndwr (c.1350–1415), or Owen Glendower, as the name is usually Anglicised, is a—perhaps *the*—Welsh national hero, the last man to claim the title of an independent Prince of Wales and for some years successful in his campaign to drive the English from his country. But in the early years of the fifteenth century he lost most of what he had gained, and according to English legend he died, a fugitive in the Welsh mountains, of starvation.

Welsh legend, however, has Glendower living into a peaceful old age in Herefordshire, in which county he is said to have died and been buried. No one knows for sure where his grave is, no one knows for sure the manner of his death. He is, though, a hero, around whom stories and legend accumulate. He may also, and justifiably, be called an adventurer. If, that is, we use the word in the sense Dr Johnson ascribes to it in his Dictionary: "he that seeks occasions of hazard; he that puts himself in the hands of chance." And in this sense the illiterate, hapless Glyndwr Michael can also legitimately be thought of as an adventurer. His fugitive days in London ended in starvation, but his body, put in the hands of chance, found adventure in Spain.

***

I wish I'd had the opportunity to talk to my parents about "Bill Martin", but I only discovered his sad, ridiculous, "heroic" story some years after they had died. I think my father's response would have been one of wry fatalism. Whatever happens, happens, he'd have said, or anyway thought. And my mother?

She, I think, would have seen in the tale evidence of how at any moment of our lives the pit can open under our feet. The precariousness of survival, of victory over evil or dire misfortune, was intrinsic to her anxious sense of what life offers. "Bill Martin's" body might after all have sunk without trace. Hitler might not have been fooled. Of course, the war would still have been won, though more lives would probably have been lost. But who could feel anything other than dismay at the presumed need to make use of someone whose own life was from the outset a terrible misfortune, who almost certainly never knew any happiness, and who died utterly alone. Such dismay, is, without doubt, what at its deepest anxiety means.

Water

As he came close to the end of the corridor, a door ahead of him to his left opened and a man stepped out. Tall, wearing a brown tweed suit that looked vaguely professorial, the man smiled. "Lost?" he asked, then, without waiting for an answer, his voice low but distinct, said, "through that door"—pointing directly across from where he stood—"down the stairs, turn left at the bottom. That will take you to the exit."

He opened his mouth to say thank you but the man had already gone back into the room and pulled the door shut behind him.

The corridor to which he had been directed was wide, parquet-floored, and sure enough at its far end he could make out a glass door through which came green-filtered light that softened the sombre, wood-panelled walls. As he walked toward the door he saw that beyond its frosted glass were the blurred shapes of bushes and trees.

But when he was within a few yards of the exit, a door, this time to his right, swung open—although unlike the one upstairs this one opened inward, as though in welcome. Though nobody emerged he became aware that an aged woman was bending to help an even older one rise from one of those collapsible wheel-chairs used to help infirm passengers onto and off trains and aeroplanes.

He quickened his step and between them he and the woman got the old lady, who was very light, up from the chair and, each with a hand under an elbow, guided her slowly and carefully through the door.

As they entered the room a much younger woman came to greet them. Tall and slim, she wore a cream silk blouse open at the neck and black, high-waisted trousers.

"Have you reserved a table?" she asked, looking from one to the other of the two women. She did not appear to take any notice of his presence, and, after registering her calm, unhurried speech, the way her soft voice seemed to match a face framed by immaculate, shoulder length curls of dark hair, he was free to gaze about him.

The restaurant was almost full, and couples leaned close together, elbows resting on the snow-white cloths as they talked intently to each other, although he could make out nothing of what they were saying. It was as if they were exchanging thoughts rather than words.

But now, having presumably guided the two elderly women to a table, for they were no longer visible, the young woman stood beside him.

"Are you planning to eat with us," she asked.

He wanted to say yes, because it had come to him that this was one of the pleasantest restaurants he had ever entered. The walls, papered in a rich, orange-red colour he thought of as Bonnard-like, made the room glow, and tendrils of vine spread across the high ceiling which was painted a delicate shade of blue. Laid out for inspection on long trestle tables were deep tureens with elaborately carved ladles beside them, cheeses and breads on trenchers, salads arranged in large glass bowls, a swan that was probably sculpted from ice, and fruits heaped up on earthenware plates. Wine bottles stood ready and open, glassware beside them, waiting.

But he had to be going.

"Well then," the young woman said, "perhaps you would like to come here some other time."

She was about to say more, he thought, but another man was now standing in front of her, claiming her attention. This one was ruddy-cheeked, sported a neat, full moustache to match his black, slicked-back hair, and although not as tall as the woman, exuded an air of confident familiarity. "I would like here to bring my Elizabeth," he said, his perfect pronunciation and slight imperfection of syntax indicated that he must be a foreigner.

He thought, yes, although I lack this man's assurance, I would like to bring *my* wife here, and the thought made him very happy.

***

Awake, he tried to make sense of the dream, but couldn't. The warmth of happiness it had brought him did not however fade. What time is it, he wondered, aware of the pitch-black bedroom. He turned to look at the illuminated face of the bedside clock. 9.

9 o'clock? That couldn't be right. Propping himself on his elbows, he peered into the dark, thinking as he did so, we came upstairs at 11 p.m. and it can't yet be morning because there are no sounds, no cars, no voices; besides if it *were* 9 o'clock light would be showing round the curtains.

Then he remembered his wife's warning about the need to replace the clock's batteries.

As he did so, he felt her stir at his side.

He eased himself down under the duvet, not wanting to wake her.

But at once, he jerked upward again, listening intently.

"What's the matter."

She was awake now, just, her voice thick with sleep.

"Can't you hear it?"

He sensed her raise her head, then let it fall back. "Hear what?"

"Water. Running water. Listen."

She moved her body closer and in the intense dark they listened, side by side. Then, wearily, she said, "I can't hear anything. You're imagining it."

He was amazed, then angered. "I'm not, of *course* I'm not. That sound is water, rushing through the pipes. Perhaps one of us left a tap on in the bathroom."

"Well, it wasn't me." He felt her turn away from him, seeking to re-enter the sleep from which he'd pulled her.

He waited for some minutes, during which the sounds that had disturbed him continued, now louder, now softer, but never dying, then, as soon as the evenness of her breathing told him she was once more asleep, he slipped from bed, felt for his bedside torch and, careful to mask its beam with a covering hand, let a sliver of light guide him to the door.

Outside, on the landing, he eased the bedroom door shut, stood listening.

Some months earlier, the water tank, which was housed in their box room, had sprung a leak. It had happened during the night, and in the morning they woke to find water seeping under their bedroom door, while, on the landing, more water eddied across the stained wood boards and slopped down the stairs. As for the ground floor, water was everywhere, furniture and rugs sodden, the newly-fitted kitchen tiles dull red under what looked like an incoming tide. In the following days many of their possessions had to go to the skip and the installation of a new tank and heating system proved costly, time-consuming, and had exhausted the patience of them both.

On the dark landing, he listened. There couldn't be another leak, could there? Please not, he thought, I couldn't bear it.

He crouched to feel the landing carpet. Dry. He crossed to the box-room, went in and, having snapped on the torch, knelt, ear pressed to the tank's cool metal. No sound came from it. The tank was fine. There was no leak.

He stood, allowed the ache in his joints to subside, turned off the light and went back out onto the landing. The sounds that had woken him had stopped.

Nevertheless, he decided that before he went back to bed he would check the new boiler.

Using his torch, he trod quietly downstairs. The system was programmed to come on at 6.30 a.m. and at this hour, whatever the hour might be, the boiler slumbered against the kitchen wall, quiescent, its unwavering blue eye assuring him that nothing was amiss. He shone his torch over the brand-new kitchen tiles, cold to his bare feet, even bent to touch them. They were bone dry. He retreated.

The bedroom door was now ajar. Even so, he pushed it no wider than allowed for him to squeeze through and, as quietly as he could, slid back into bed. But when he reached for his wife it was as he thought. She had left the bed. He smiled to think that while he was gone she must have woken and, unaware that he was downstairs, tiptoed from the bedroom, wanting not to wake him, then, as so often when she couldn't sleep, made her way into the spare bedroom for a few hours' rest before returning to the marriage bed.

***

When he next woke grey light was leaking round the curtains. The radio alarm, timed to come on at 7 a.m., was announcing that the news would follow immediately. He reached to switch it off and noticed that it was indeed showing 7. The clock had somehow righted itself.

Only then did he turn to see that his wife had not after all come back to bed. For once she must have fallen into a prolonged sleep in what they called their guest room—though truth to tell there were no longer many friends or relations to take advantage of their hospitality.

He climbed stiffly from bed and reached for his dressing-gown. He would make tea for them both.

Before going downstairs he carefully turned the knob of the closed guest room door, and eased it open. Should she still be slumbering he had no wish to wake her. Let her sleep on.

But the bed was unused.

In her wakefulness she must have gone downstairs to the lounge, probably to read, and then fallen asleep on the sofa. It had been known.

But she wasn't there, either. The sofa, like the bed in the guest room, was unoccupied, nor was there any sign that his wife had used it. No book, open or closed, lay beside the sofa, no cushion had been used as a pillow, nor had the curtains, drawn back when they went to bed the previous evening, been closed against the night.

Opening the kitchen door he saw that she was lying full length beside the boiler and even before he knelt beside her he knew that she was dead.

"Elizabeth," he said, but pressing his palm against her ice-cold forehead he had to accept that she had been lying there for many hours.

It's None of Your Business

Why the delay?

Oh, of course. Because it was Saturday morning. On any other day of the week she could step into the newsagent's, buy her paper, and be back home at her desk before her coffee had cooled.

But Saturday was different. Saturday was queue-day. A line of men and women patiently standing, or shifting from foot to foot in various degrees of irritation, some there to pay bills, others, the majority, waiting to buy scratch cards or lottery tickets, or both, men and women of all ages dreaming of a fortune—"we shan't let it spoil our lives"—and already imagining a house in the country, explosions of champagne, the four-wheel drive, business-class seats on intercontinental airbuses, all those glittering prizes, the promise of which required them to stand here, heads bowed in penitential silence, as if determined to avoid the mutual acknowledgement of guilt which eye contact would entail. As if....

But this Saturday the queue was moving more slowly than usual. Oh, get on with it.

Although Kate had certainly not spoken the words aloud, the woman immediately ahead of her, a large, shapeless figure in a heavily belted raincoat, turned, raising an eyebrow and sighing extravagantly. "Anyone'd think we'd got all day."

Kate smiled in sympathy. "A log jam. I wonder what's causing it?"

And at once, a voice, a man's voice, raised as if in answer to her question, came from the front of the queue. "I tell you it's *art*, you stupid woman." Then, volume down though still audible this far back, the words, more measured, but vibrant with anger, "Not that it's any of your damned business."

Heads were raised, the queue rippled. Wind travelling through corn.

Edging a little out of line in order to look beyond the woman who was now turned in the direction of the voice, Kate saw his back as he loomed above the counter. Tall, longish black hair curled over the collar of a brown cord jacket that for a heart-jolting moment reminded her.... Though it wasn't him. Of course it wasn't.

She took a deep breath, made herself attend to his words, the exasperated emphases, the suggestion of frustrated, baffled authority.

"It's *not* pornography, you stupid, *stupid* woman, it's *art*."

Something about the way he uttered the words suggested more than mere outrage. "If I wanted porn I'd go for the top shelf of this bloody shop. You've got enough of it stacked up there."

And now he was raising an arm, stabbing the air with an outstretched finger, as he pointed at a row of glossy magazines high to his left.

Others in the queue were turning to look at the shelf, its displays of prawn pink fleshiness, but she kept her eyes on what was happening at the counter.

The assistant, a short, round-faced woman whose black-rimmed spectacles and close-cropped badly-dyed black hair gave her the look of a dyspeptic chipmunk, was studying the paper in front of her. "I'm entitled to my opinion."

"*Of course* you're not." And now both arms were raised as he appealed to the heavens. "To have an *opinion* you'd have to know what you're talking about. And you *don't*."

"I'm talking about what's wrong," the woman said doggedly. She made no attempt to lower her voice, was, if anything, speaking even more loudly than the customer when she said, "And this is... is *filth*."

Kate watched the woman, in her uniform of dark-blue jacket over white blouse, rap on the counter with her knuckles, saw how finally she raised her eyes, looked briefly at the man, then away, preferring to study the lower racks of journals, weeklies, Guides to Home and Garden, Country Houses....

"Oh, *keep* the sodding thing, I'll buy elsewhere."

Turning and brushing past those immediately behind him, the man, as he came toward where Kate, still out of line, was forced to swerve round her.

Meeting her gaze, he shrugged, miming bewildered despair, then shook his head, as though inviting her to share his sense of furious incomprehension.

She followed his movements as he shouldered his way to the door, yanked it open, then, after looking up at the sky as in one last, wondering appeal to heavenly justice, disappeared into the thronged street. Through the door, which he hadn't bothered to close, a cold breeze came to disturb newspapers and customers alike.

"Why doesn't someone shut the damned thing?"

Kate looked briefly at the man behind her who had spoken the words, marched to the door, shut it, and returned to her place in the queue.

The raincoated woman, having turned once more to Kate, nodded and smiled her approval. "Some people," she said, raising an eyebrow, though Kate had no idea whether she was referring to the man who had stormed out of the shop or the one who hadn't thought it his place to shut the door. Both perhaps.

A few minutes later, waiting at the counter for change from the note she had handed over, she glanced at the journal Mr Angry had thrown down, now spread across the counter's wooden surface. It was this week's *Times Literary Supplement*. Featured on its cover was the reproduction of a picture she knew and loved. A group of nude women dancing in a ring. The dancers, cut out of pink paper, formed a simple, frieze-like image. Matisse at his most decoratively joyous.

Noticing Kate's glance, the assistant said, as she handed over the money, "No wonder teenagers nowadays are like—like animals. Giving them this kind of thing to look at." The truculence in her voice was threaded through with a mute appeal. Woman to woman.

Kate looked again and as she did so realisation dawned. "This isn't the *EDUCATIONAL Supplement*."

Though, supposing it had been, she ought to have added, it's not read by kids, you know, but by their teachers. And anyway....

The assistant, tears glittering behind her spectacles, sniffed. "What's the difference," she said. "It's all filth."

***

It was no more than fifty yards from the newsagent's to her preferred coffee-house. Kate took a large cup of cappuccino over to an unoccupied table and settled down to the business of discarding most sections of the *Guardian*. An indecisive moment—I will *not* look—and then she opened the book pages.

Biographies, Celebrity Memoirs, Travel. Her pulse quickened. *This Week's Fiction.* You never knew.

"Mind if I sit here."

Looking up, she saw the jeans, brown cord jacket, then his face, dark-jowled, full lips, nose straight though ending in a sudden blunt, cut-off point, the deep-brown eyes, black, curly hair, younger than he'd seemed in the newsagent's. Mid-thirties, no older. No, not at all like Andrew. For this relief....

"The place is pretty full."

He was offering the words as explanation, even apology—sorry, I don't mean to invade your space—though a glance around told her that there were plenty of empty chairs.

She gestured at the chair he had half-drawn out. "Of course. I mean, please."

He sat, looked up from the black coffee he'd placed in front of him, met her eyes. "It *was* you I saw in the newsagent's?"

Again she nodded, by now forlornly certain that she wasn't going to come across what earlier she had hoped, or possibly dreaded, to find there. Next week, perhaps. These were early days.

He watched her push the pages aside, raised an eyebrow in mute enquiry.

"My lottery ticket," she said. "Nothing in it for me, I'm afraid. No promise of a yacht in the Med."

He waited for her to explain, and only when, after a moment's prolonged silence, he saw she wasn't going to add to the remark, he said, "I owe you an apology."

"Really? Why?" She was genuinely puzzled.

"My row with that bloody woman. Holding up the queue."

"We all had to wait in line. You owe us *all* an apology."

"True." He laughed, looked round at the tables, studied the queue at the bar. Then he turned back to her. "But as far as I can see you're the only one present to whom I can say sorry."

After a moment or two, during which he took a sip of coffee before, using both hands, he carefully lowered the cup to its saucer, he said, "I suppose I shouldn't have lost my temper?"

She surprised herself by agreeing. "No, you shouldn't."

It wasn't the answer he had expected. Startled, his anticipatory smile gone, he looked from her to the review pages she was now folding into the pocket of her coat. "I see. So can I ask you, what would *you* have done?"

She considered. "I'd have tried to find a way of suggesting it was none of her business but without humiliating her. Without being offensive."

He pretended to consider this. "I can't imagine a way of telling anyone that something isn't their business without sounding offensive."

"Oh, I think it can be done."

He drank his coffee, put the cup firmly down and said, "OK. Show me."

He was challenging her, the slight smile suggesting a sceptical disbelief.

She looked away, then back, in role. "That's none of your business, I'm afraid," she said, emphasising the word *afraid* and, as she did so, smiling. A disarming smile, collusive, a smile intended to invite a measure of sympathetic understanding.

A moment's reflection, then, "That's brilliant," he said, bringing his hands together in silent applause. He leant back in his chair. "I'm genuinely impressed. Are you an actress? I mean actor."

She allowed herself a brief, terse, smile. "No."

She finished her cappuccino, and wanting now to leave, reached down for her shoulder bag.

"What then? If you don't mind telling me, that is." He was trying to keep her talking.

She finished folding her newspaper into her bag, raised her eyes to meet his gaze. "Suppose you first tell me what *you* do?"

His smile challenged her. "Guess. I mean, I guessed *your* profession, line of work—wrongly, I admit, but I tried."

His words, no, the look that accompanied them, nettled her. Bet you can't guess. Or, bet you'll be impressed when you know.

"Teacher," she said, "university lecturer, probably. Professor, even?" She pushed back her chair and stood. An end to this. He no longer interested her. He had so little to offer.

He held up his hands in mock surrender. "Got me bang to rights. How did you work it out?"

Because of your dress, she might have said, but more particularly because you were enjoying yourself in that row in the newsagent's. Because you think yourself a justified putter-down of the great unwashed, because your smile is the kind for which the word smug might have been invented.

But she said nothing, though she gave him a final, brief look, knowing how she could make use of him. She might even call him Andrew. But first she had to finish her shopping.

So when, as she buttoned her coat, ready to leave, and he asked, casually but with intent, whether she might perhaps be free later on, it was easy to reply, "That's none of your business, I'm afraid."

And this time she wasn't smiling.

To Avoid Those Eyes

All I'm trying to say is that poetry may help, but it isn't what gets you through life. I mean, bread before ballads, vino before villanelles, that's my motto. Mince before Marvell? Yes, that's good. How about sherry before Shakespeare? No, you're right, sherry rots the guts. As for malt doing more than Milton can to justify God's ways to Man, I don't buy it. Why not? Because quite a few of my friends have gone up the chimney through too much intake of malt, that's why not. Yes, alright Housman wasn't thinking of whisky, but I am. Malt whisky did for them all. I don't see much justification in that, do you? Not unless God's some sort of Manichee. You know, embodiment of an evil spirit. Malt, the evil spirit. That would make sense.

But this may interest you. You don't mind me nattering on, do you? I mean, I saw you were holding a "slim volume", as the saying goes, and thought, aha, another addict. None of the others seem to be reading much apart from tourist guides. Besides, they've got each other. Here for the views, I guess. That and the ozone. Too cold for a swim this time of year, though. I guess that's why the package was so cheap. Like this coffee. Cheap and weak. The waiter must have shown the bean a jug of hot water and it died of fright.

What was I saying? Ah, yes. I once came across a poem called *National Poetry Day*. On the back of a postcard, sent by someone I used to know, though the less said about her—about *that*—the better. *National Poetry Day*. I ask you. Some bloody silly encomium to the essential role poetry ought to play in all our lives, I thought, some feelgood lines about how we're bound to die miserably without its tender ministrations. Poetry as celebration of spiritual values, of eternal verities, of the big questions. As if the shiftless wonders I've occasionally knocked up against would be capable of raising *any* question beyond who's going to pay for the next round or volunteer to act as sounding board while they complain about the tossers with a personal grudge against them, which is the only explanation there can *possibly* be for why their last book got universally trashed.

But then I read the poem. And I thought, well, good for you, mate. Because it was about how poetry can and probably will muck up your life. "*Transform your life with poetry.*" The Scottish Book Trust dreamt up that slogan for National Poetry Day. So this poet, Gael Turnbull, who was apparently a doctor "in real life", pretends he thinks the claim's a bit over the top. But hang on. Poetry, our Gael remembers, "*had thrust/ several old friends,/ plus near and dear,/ into distress and penury.*" So he decides that the Book Trust must be issuing "*a sort of timely/ Health Warning.*"

Bloody good. I like it. Why? Well, because speaking personally, as I believe we're encouraged to do when discussing poetry, Mr Turnbull got it in one. Poetry *is* a disaster area. There now. That's the truth. No, not sour grapes, on my mother's grave. Yes, I admit that in my youth I tried my hand at it. Don't we all? I even sent off some of what I fondly imagined was deathless stuff to magazines. Needless to say, back it all came. Well, not all, in fact not much. I never heard from most of the places I sent to, even though I always took good care to enclose an sae. Par for the course, some greybeard told me later. Apparently magazine editors are in the habit of using the stamped envelopes, suitably re-addressed, to send out their own bloody poems. Still, I kept the comments that came from those who bothered to provide any. All the way from the full eloquence of "Sorry not for us" to "Why not try the Samaritans." You know George Shearing's remark that "Lullaby of Birdland" apart, he'd composed some two hundred and fifty numbers which all made the bumpy journey from obscurity to oblivion? My story more or less, though I gave up long before I'd got to 250 rejections.

But as I say, it's not sour grapes I'm spitting out. The fact is poetry only did me harm *after* I stopped trying to write it. Ain't that a kick in the head, as Fred MacMurray might have said, as he did in fact say when his wife booted him out. Yes, *The Apartment*. One of the great films. Pure poetry. Ha!

Transform your life with poetry. Well, my first wife gave me the old heave-ho when I read her a poem, can you believe? Some transformation *that* proved to be. I mean there I was thinking I'd got the perfect marriage. Sweet romance followed by the parade up the aisle, two kids in four years, nice house, steady job, what more could anyone want?

Answer, poetry. One evening, there was nothing on the box, she'd finished her library book, so I volunteered to read to her. She said she'd like that. Yes, well.

Of all the poems of all the books on all the shelves in the world I chose one by Robert Graves. A favourite poet, I told her. One of the causes of my addiction, Mr Graves. He dealt in poetry, pure and unadulterated. Every one a winner, so which poem to try? Now, hear this. I decided on "With her Lips Only". What a choice!

If you don't know it, I'll give you a brief resumé. It begins with this woman, an "honest wife" according to our poet, meeting a lover at the garden gate one evening, as you do. He wants the pair of them to effect a disappearing act but she refuses. Her conscience won't let her, because of the children. Next stanza, switch of scene. She's in bed being "challenged" by her husband to have sex and she thinks she must, "*for the children's sake,*" only as she thinks this she turns "*suddenly cold towards them.*" Graves's own words.

Not exactly an endorsement of married love, I admit, but a good poem, an unrhymed sonnet, as I took care to explain.

But she wasn't interested in that.

"You've been spying on me," she said. "You vengeful bastard."

You don't need me to spell it out, do you? Seems she'd been having an affair with the next-door-but-one. I hadn't a clue, of course. At least, that's what I tell myself, although I sometimes wonder what led me to choose that particular poem. Anyway, next thing the perfect marriage is no more, she clears off with the bloke and kids in tow, and I'm on my own.

God, this coffee. Too early for anything alcoholic, I suppose. No, no chance, I can see that at a glance. Lockdown time at the bar for a further hour or several. So, poetry. You'd have thought that the experience with Graves might have taught me my lesson. But no, addicts rarely kick the habit. "Once Bitten, Twice Bitten", as some other poet has it. The same poet who got me into trouble the next time.

Ah, yes. Second marriages, the triumph of hope over experience, except there wasn't much by way of triumph in mine and hope took an early bath. Probably why we decided on a holiday in the sun. You know, Lanzarotte will put the zing back into your love life. Ha! I don't know what made me pack *Preaching to the Converted*, but there I was, on the beach, telling her to listen while, for a laugh, I read her "Sex and the Over Forties." "*Back to the dream in the garden,/ back to the pictures in the drawer,/ back to back, tonight and every night.*"

The closing lines. I remember them just like I remember her response. Worked her way out of the deckchair, says, "Well, I prefer front to front," and by the time I got back to the hotel she'd packed and left. So that was the end to Marriage Numero Two.

Christ, this is depressing, isn't it. Let's change the subject. Or, as they say in the films, that's quite enough about me, tell me about yourself. That book you were reading when I joined you, who's it by, may I ask? Fleur Adcock? Yes, I think I've heard of her. *High Tide in the Garden*. Can I have a look? You've got the marker here, at this poem. Yes, this one. "Against Coupling."

"*Five minutes of solitude/ are enough—in the bath, or to fill/ that gap between the Sunday papers and lunch.*"

Oh, I see.

Right, I think I'll take a stroll. I'm told the headland over there has a few pairs of breeding puffins I could look at. Enjoy your book. And if we meet again before the end of the week, perhaps I could buy you a drink? If not, well, *c'est la vie*, as I suppose some poet must sometime have said.

The Goods

Well, since we're talking bass players and the like, let me tell you about Gamp and Harris. Not their real names, by the way, but what they were called on the circuit. Being as how you're from out of town, I guess you won't know about them? No, I thought not. Which means that you won't have heard them in action. A pity, that, a great pity, you being a bass man yourself. Yeh, you'll get to spell ours, no problem. Buy him a pint and he'll probably let you have the whole of the middle set. I take it you wouldn't object? Still, no need to be this early to stake a claim. I prefer getting one or two down before the music starts, sort of anaesthetises the pain, but it's not like old times, if you know what I mean. Back in the day even local groups could fill a place. And for a London band, it was be here for opening time or don't bother. But not now. Take a look around. Half an hour to curtain up and the place is still empty. No, I'm always first in. The rest of the outfit will be along soon as they've ironed their trusses.

Yes, right. I'm on trombone. As you so rightly observe, the case is a give-away. Used to play a bit with Gamp and Harris, *if* we could get them. Looked forward to those occasions, everyone did, they gave any band they played with a lift. I'm not saying they were world beaters. Not Walter Page and Philly-Jo. Not even nationally known, though more than a few of us reckon they should have been. They could have shown the way to some of the Mr. Bigs from down London.

Like? Well, for instance like... No, better not. No names, no pack drill. Let's just say that either of them was an asset to any band you'd care to hear, and not just on a wet Monday night in Arnold. But put them together, as they always liked to be, and then you'd got something special. One plus one makes four.

Yes, *of course* they should have been better known. But they didn't like to travel, simple as that. Well, to be straight, Harry wouldn't have minded, but Dave said no. And his thumbs-down put the kibosh on gigs far from home.

Anyway, to fill you in. Harry Silver played bass, Dave Gams was a drummer, and like most semi-pros they hung on to the day job. Harry cut hair in a gents saloon run by an old mate from army days. *CLEAN CUT* it was called. Original or what? But as Harry said, it took care of the bills.

Dave was his own boss. A bits and pieces man. Ran errands for anyone who'd pay him to ferry goods from pillar to post. In heavy demand, too, and he kept his van spotless, engine always in good nick, gears smooth as a Buck Clayton lick, up early and out; but by the end of each and every day he'd had enough of driving. That's why they only ever did gigs in and around the city. The van wasn't going anywhere that Dave didn't want to go, and he didn't want to go more than ten miles from home, fifteen at most, and then only for what my old ma would have called a king's ransom. So after a while band leaders out of Nottingham stopped bothering. I mean, there's always someone else to hire.

You'd see Dave's van about town any day of the week. *GAMS HOME DELIVERIES*. Dave got the lettering done professionally. Black on white. Very tasty, he reckoned. *GAMS HOME DELIVERIES*. That's how they got to be called Harris and Gamp. Mr Gamp, someone started calling Dave. Very droll. Get it? Gamp—home deliveries? OK. And then, because he and Harry were mates who always used Dave's van to get to gigs, Harry became Mr. Harris.

If they minded they never said so. They may not even have got the joke, not until it was explained to them, and anyway they liked jokes. Well, some of them. Yes, it's true, drummers do get picked on. Who do drummers like to hang out with? Musicians—that kind of thing. Bass players have it easier, though apparently not in the world of what we used to call "longhair" music, where the players all went to college and learned to hold their sheet music the right way up. You've probably heard the one about the concert where the orchestra takes an interval break and the leader of the second violins discovers the bass player huddled in a corner. "What's up?" "The oboist untuned one of my strings," the bass player tells him. "Well, re-tune it." "But he won't tell me which one it is." Yes, a banjo joke in the jazz world, I know, I know. Old as pre-electric records.

Old jokes didn't worry Gamp and Harris. The older the better. Harry told jokes while he cut hair. Any road, he told the one. You must have heard it, though no doubt the name of the place would have been changed. In Harry's version some bloke goes into the barber's in Sandiacre. "I want my hair cut like Frank Sinatra," he tells the barber. "Can you manage that?" "Certainly, sir," the barber says. "Take a seat and we'll soon have you looking the very image of Ol' Blue Eyes." So the bloke sits down, sheet's tucked round him, out come the scissors, snip, snip, snip, snip. Ten minutes later the barber says, "Right, job done, and to your satisfaction I trust," handing the client a mirror. Client takes one look and yells "That's not how Frank Sinatra has his hair cut!" "It is when he comes here," the barber says.

Harry must have told that plenty of times between nine to five while he was making with the short back and sides. And Dave, he was quick with the chat. Always had a line to offer the ladies. Bringing in a chair or table he's carted over from an antique shop. "Any other way I can service you, I mean be of service. If you think of something, give me a bell and I'm all yours."

Whether he got anything out of it I doubt, but I never heard that anyone took offence. Anyway, unlike Harry, Dave wasn't married. Harry's wife, Enid, now, she was a lovely lady. Used to sing a bit with various groups, especially if Harry and Dave were on stand, but then she retired from what she called the high life of Mansfield Working Men's Club and settled for part-time work as a barwoman. Always well turned out, and she'd still sometimes be with them on a gig, sing a couple, "Summertime," "Ghost of a Chance," say, but eventually she packed it in. Reckoned her voice couldn't stand the pace. Stayed loyal to the bar work, though.

Like I say, Dave wasn't married. Didn't even have a steady woman, just the one-nighters or, as someone said, the one-afternooners. If that. 'Course, you heard rumours. But as I say, I doubt Dave was the gigolo some claimed. Not that the image did him any harm and off stand he was the one who always got the ladies' attention. Bit of a natty dresser, smiled a lot, never without a word, whereas Harry tended to keep the lip buttoned.

But on stand it was all change. Depending on the music, Harry could do you "Papa Slow Drag", a more-than-passable imitation of Blanton, and, when the mood took him, shut your eyes and you'd swear you were listening to Slam Stewart. You don't often hear bass players being applauded, do you? Well, *you'd* know. But they'd put their hands together for Harry, *and* without being asked.

Now here's a funny thing. Take a deep breath. Dave was the reverse. Mr Invisible. What, I hear you ask, a drummer dodging the limelight? Difficult to credit, I'll grant you, but it's true. Never went further than an eight-bar break. Apart from that he handled the traps so you didn't know he was there until he stopped playing. *Then* you noticed. He was ace on brushes. Lovely light touch. Harris and Gamp. I'm telling you, together they were the best round here by a long chalk, they really were. Anyone starting a band wanted those two.

Mind, Harry had a bit of back problem. Someone wondered whether that came from leaning over to whisper in a customer's ear. You know, "Something for the weekend?" or "A little bird told me about a cert for the 2.15 at Haydock Park." But Harry said, no. It was an occupational hazard of bass players. Being on your legs for hours at a time, leaning at an odd angle to get at the strings.

Yes, thanks. Just a half.

Well, all musos have their problems. With guitarists it's arthritic fingers, which can also get to keyboard players. Brass, the lip goes. Reeds are OK but there are other deficiencies. You know the old joke about the salesman in the bar who could talk to anyone on their own level? Taps one bloke on the shoulder. Can I ask your IQ? 200. No sweat. Ten minutes on astrophysics, giving as good as he gets. Tries the next bloke. 150. So they talk geo-politics. Then he asks a third. "My IQ is 35," he's told. "That so?" the salesman says. "So what reeds do you use?"

It depends on who's telling the joke, of course. But you wouldn't do a take-down joke about bass players or drummers, not to Harris and Gamp, you wouldn't. Well out of order. Not that they came on as prima donnas. Solid citizens, the pair of them. Always on time, dressed to rules, whether it was a black-and-white job or scruff order, and *never* drink taken. I mean, some musos are on the wild side. And not just because of the booze or nose powder. It seems to go with the territory. Knives, for instance. Mingus, Dizzy Gillespie in his younger days. He carried a knife, did you know that?

No, can't say I've come across anyone wielding steel in these parts, but guns, yes. When the lads came back after 1945 there were plenty of service revolvers came with them. And of course Bechet was a hero. "Les Oignons", "The Fish Seller", "Petite Fleur". You wouldn't get through an evening without playing at least one of them. He'd been deported from England in the early 20s, as I expect you know, then Germany. They put him on trial in 1929, Frankfurt I think it was, for perforating a pianist's kneecap. His defence—defence mark you—was that he'd been aiming at the banjoist. Ah, banjoist jokes. What's the difference between a chiropodist and a banjoist? A chiropodist bucks up the feet. And there's the one about the muso who turns up at Ronnie Scott's for a gig. Ronnie points at the case he's carrying. "What the hell's in *that?*" our Ronald asks. "Semtex," the muso says. "Thank God," Ronnie tells him. "I thought it might be a banjo."

Sure, there are still a few wild men in England, not as many as in Scotland, it's true. Find yourself on the receiving end of a Glasgow kiss and it can take weeks before your lip heals. You don't get that here, not in good old Nottingham, though I've seen a couple with guns in their waistbands, fantasists dreaming that Bulwell is Basin Street. One was up from Kent. Claimed Chatham Dockyard was like the waterfront down in Delta City. Dream on! Dapper Dan he was called, on account of his dress. Three-piece suits with high waistband, tan brogues, and a heavy black coat draped over his shoulders even in warm weather. Came complete with snap-brim trilby and fat cigar, bought from his takings as a bookie's runner. Always stood at the bar, and only drank rum. One night he must have had one or several too many because right after a gig at his local he loosed off his shooter, and all the shop alarms started up like it was early closing in Hell. By the time the old Bill came looking we had him wedged under a bar table but next day Dapper Dan was strongly advised to return himself to from whence he came. He's back here now, I'm told, suits and all, but minus the shooter.

Harris and Gamp were on that particular gig, guesting, helping to put bums on seats. In fact it was Dave's kit, heaped round the table, that kept Dapper Dan from the prying eyes of the boys in blue.

Harris and Gamp. They'd play with any band, never bothered too much about the money, they loved playing.

Well, there was an exception, one outfit they avoided if they could—we all did. You won't have heard of Ron Wardell, will you? Trumpet man. No, well, good, keep it that way. The emphasis is on the second syllable. War*dell*. Known locally as Ron Wardell and His Music from Hell. It was, too. RW could only play in two keys: B flat and F. "Play" is a bit of an over-statement, by the way, like calling the Gobi Desert a deepwater lake.

No, it's my shout. Landlord? Same again, please.

Where was I? Oh, yes. RW But if he was *that* bad, you're no doubt wondering, how come he got any work? Undercutting others, that's how. He was a crafty sod, I'll say that for him. Soon as he heard of a new place opening up he'd be round to see the manager. "Have you hired a band yet? Really? How much you paying them? That's too much. They're robbing you blind. Tell you what, I'll put in a group for £50 less."

That's how RW got the jobs. It usually meant that opening night coincided with closing night. Sometimes it didn't even take *that* long. One of the lads reckons that the record for RW being invited to sling his hook was half-an-hour, by which time most of the punters had left, those who hadn't been forewarned, that is. The latter were the lucky ones, took an evening off, put their feet up and spent a few hours in front of the tele. Some used to wonder how the old bugger was able to get away with it for so long. I put it down to the greed and stupidity of managers, plus a muso or two in need of money who could actually play, as a result of which RW's band would occasionally sound only a bit south of bloody awful.

Anyway, to get to the point. One night RW was booked to open at a pub-restaurant some way out of town. For once he'd even managed to put together a decent line-up, himself excepted, but there was a little problem. The drummer and bass player were coming down from Sunderland. RW hadn't asked Harris and Gamp, he knew they'd say no, but then everyone else local turned him down. Drummers discovered a subsequent engagement or were away for a month, burying an old grannie in Utrecht, bass players he tried were sorry but, would you credit it, the instrument was in for long-term repair, and, no, it was impossible to borrow one.

Luckily for RW, his reputation hadn't yet spread to Sunderland. Maybe it was stopped at the Humber, prevented from going further, put into quarantine, I don't know. Anyway, the agency he went through had had word there were musos up there gagging for work, so they got on the blower and managed to reel in two-thirds of a rhythm section from what was known to be a more than average group.

But then, half an hour before starter's orders, the pub fields a phone call. There's been a crash on the M1, traffic backed up, nothing moving and won't be for several hours. You can kiss goodbye to the lads from Sunderland making the gig.

So what does RW do? Of course! Puts out a May Day call to Harris and Gamp. He tries Dave's place first. After all, Dave's the wheels. No answer. Harry's next up.

Enid answers. She's in a hurry, she tells him, works on a Tuesday night, or had he forgotten. But anyway she can't be doing with his pestering her. "They're on your gig or had you forgotten that too? They left here an hour ago which means they'll be with you in the next few minutes." And with that she slams the phone down.

Well, RW, who everyone reckons is a few bricks short of a load, though not when it comes to muscling in on someone else's gig, at first thinks thank God for that. We'll be OK. Job saved.

But then it comes to him. An hour earlier Harris and Gamp couldn't have known they'd be wanted for the gig. As far as they and anyone else knew, it was Sunderland to the rescue. So what's going on?

The question must have been agitating both halves of his one working brain cell an hour later when there was still no sign of

Harris and Gamp and the management, having listened to the band, such as it was—and there's not much you can do with three front-line and a guitarist, especially if the trumpet lead sounds like a bullfrog with the runs—had given RW his marching orders. RW always maintained that if he'd had a full rhythm section that night he'd have got a regular booking. And Russ Conway is Teddy Wilson.

Of course, the story of what happened or rather *didn't* happen that night got around. It was bound to. But here's the funny thing. Neither Harris nor Gamp said anything. Wouldn't so much as mention it. Not a peep, nothing. Schtum. Silent as the grave they were.

A bit weird, that. At first some of us tried asking, but we soon gave up. They'd shrug and turn away, or just stare at you. I mean, there's only so many times you can stand to get what Benny Goodman's sidemen used to call "the ray," you know, the look he sent someone who hit a bum note or missed an intro. Not well-loved, Goodman. You hear the one about a couple of musos who bump into one another on Broadway, and one asks the other "You want the good news or the bad?" "The good." "Benny Goodman's dead." "So what's the bad news?" "He died peacefully."

But we all liked Harris and Gamp. They were good mates with most of us. That was what made it odd. Why the looks? The heavy silences? There were those who reckoned Enid was covering up for Harry. He was there all the time and she knew he wouldn't want to spend an evening in RW's company. But that doesn't explain why Dave didn't answer *his* phone. Well, he could have been out, though if so it wasn't on any other gig, because that night, as it happened, there weren't any other gigs, not in our area, and, like I say, Dave never travelled. If the job wasn't on his doorstep, so to speak, he wasn't prepared to take it.

Makes you wonder, doesn't it? Someone dropped a rumour that the two were involved in a dodgy deal. Liberating metal for scrap, say, or disposing of smokes or booze they'd come by in a parked-up trailer. There was a lot of that going on at the time. But it didn't seem likely. Harry in particular was Mr Reliable, and not only at four-to-the-bar. He was an honest man, I'm sure of that. It's possible that Dave didn't always ask many questions about the goods he was carrying, but I'm positive Harry kept his own nose clean and I don't see Dave risking anything, not with Harry alongside.

Do I have an explanation? No, I don't. There *was* a whisper that maybe Harry and Dave were a bit, you know, that way inclined, and that they'd crept off to some hotel or were parked up in a lay-by for a spot of how's your father. Not that it makes any odds. I mean, what counts is the music, and, like I say, those two were ace.

Yes, the past tense. You noticed. It all finished when Dave died a few years ago, got his van smashed into by some dozy truck driver who'd been on the road for too many hours and gone to sleep at the wheel. After that, Harry never played again. End of Harris and Gamp.

Did we try to get him back on stand? You bet we did. He was quality. I know for a fact several outfits offered him top dollar, but no dice, he wouldn't be tempted. Said his back was too bad. The last I heard, he and Enid had left town. Someone said that their marriage had gone downhill, she'd been seen with one of the bar staff at the place she worked evenings, but I wouldn't know. I only know that he was a damn good bass player. As Dave was a damn good drummer. Right out of the ordinary, those two, top drawer.

The goods? Yes, I like it. They were the goods, alright. I'll drink to that.

The Furies

Watching until the police car pulled out of the close, Marie waved after it one more time, then closed the front door.

"I thought that went pretty well," she said, as she rejoined her friends in the front room.

"It went *very* well," Alice said. The two of them exchanged approving smiles.

Nodding enthusiastically, Pearl, sitting beside Alice on the sofa, also smiled. "Do let us help you with the tea-things," she said, labouring to prise herself up from the sofa's soft depths.

"There's really no need." Marie knelt to stack used cups and saucers that were strewn across the low table and, taking up plates one by one, shook crumbs from them onto the emptied cake stand. Specks that had fallen into the dark green carpet she tweezered between thumb and forefinger.

"Nimbler on your pins than I am," Alice said, following Marie's movements. Bracing herself against the sofa arm, she, too, struggled upright.

"They liked your sponge," Pearl said.

Marie tried not to notice the smear of gooseberry jam above her friend's uncertainly lipsticked mouth, the shaking hands with which Pearl attempted to position the stand on the tray. When she had finally succeeded, she patted her chest as you would an obedient dog.

"I don't suppose they get much of that kind of thing nowadays," Alice said. "Home-made cake, I mean." Having waved her hostess back, she lifted the wicker tray by its handles, straightening slowly as she did so. "Carefully does it," she said, rotating her head in order to stare at Marie and Pearl through spectacles that had slipped to the end of her nose. "Telly coppers seem to spend all their time eating burgers and drinking coffee from paper cups."

"No wonder they all look so overweight," Pearl said reprovingly.

"That's only on TV." Marie watched anxiously as Alice manoeuvred her bulk toward the door. Could Alice actually *see* the tray uncertainly balanced below her bosom's shelf? A moment later they heard the clink and rattle as, on the other side of the dividing wall, the tray was deposited on the kitchen table.

Marie held back a sigh of relief. "After all," she said to Pearl, "the policemen who were here looked quite slim, both of them."

"Who looked quite slim?" Alice said, reappearing, and tugging at the lovat green slacks that stretched uncomfortably tight around her crotch.

"The policemen. The ones who were here," Marie said. "Pearl thinks all policemen are fat but I said that it's only TV policemen who are overweight."

"I've known some pretty porky ones in my time," Alice said, falling back into the sofa, a movement which caused Pearl's body to rise involuntarily from its cushion.

"Well," Marie said, "if we're going down memory lane perhaps we should have a drink to sustain us en route."

"What a lovely idea," Pearl said uncertainly. But Alice, with unguarded enthusiasm, almost chortled. "An *excellent* notion."

At that moment the carriage clock on the marble-top fireplace began to chime.

"Six o'clock," Alice said, "smack on cue. The sun is over the yard arm, as Ginger used to say."

"A six o'clock sherry," Pearl said, and giggled.

Alice turned to look at her. There was a pause before she said, "Six o'clock sherry. Reminds me of Betjeman," nodding as though to indicate that her friend's appearance, her grey pleated skirt, the dark blue cardigan above it, papery-pale face and grey, thin hair, confirmed the likeness.

"In a way," Marie said, "although I *think* his tipple was lime juice and gin. Six o'clock gin." She crossed to the elaborately-carved sideboard on which were clustered framed family photographs and, behind them, a hanging tapestry of some hunting scene where dogs disposed themselves randomly among slender trees and a half-naked woman stood poised, bow straining to release the arrow which pointed in the direction of an antlered stag, its head lowered over water.

"Easier to rhyme, I suppose," Alice said, her remark hinting critical disapproval, and watching as Marie, having stooped to fetch a bottle from the sideboard's interior, tucked it under her arm, then with her free arm once more delved in the sideboard's depths for glasses which, as she brought them out, one by one, she held up to the light. "They look clean enough," their hostess said.

"Skerry," Pearl said, reflectively, gazing at Marie as she deposited the bottle on the table between them.

Marie stopped in the act of prising up the bottle's cork. "Skerry?" she asked, nonplussed.

"It rhymes with sherry."

"I don't know about *that*," Alice said in a manner that suggested she was far from happy with Pearl's sudden discovery of rhyme, but watching attentively as Marie began to fill the glasses. Having reached for one, she sniffed the liquid before sipping warily at it. Her look relaxed. The sherry passed muster. "I mean, Pearl, what exactly *is* a skerry?"

"It's Scottish, I believe." Pearl sounded hesitant. She smiled her silent thanks to Marie as she was handed a glass, and looked sideways at Alice, perhaps hoping her friend would accept the disapproval her glance implied. It's rude to snatch. But Alice, head well back, was emptying the glass's contents into her throat.

To Marie, Pearl said, "Ralph took me on a fishing holiday once in the Orkneys and I seem to recall that the locals called some of the islands skerries." She sipped tinily. "Oh, full cream. I'm so glad. Dry makes me liverish." She lowered the virtually untouched glass to her lap. "Still," she said, "I suppose skerries don't really apply in Leicestershire."

"No, they don't," Alice said, "though as a conversation stopper it takes some beating." But she laughed as she spoke, and, having put the glass firmly down on the table, patted her friend's arm reassuringly.

Sitting opposite them in the shabby, sagging, plum-coloured chair that she could never bring herself to throw out, Marie said, "I propose a toast." But seeing the pointed look Alice directed at her empty glass, she said, "Oh. I see a refill is called for."

When she had settled back in her chair she raised her glass and said "To us."

"To us." There was a modest exultance in the ragged chorus.

The three of them drank, though again Pearl did little more than peck at her drink.

Holding her glass at eye level, Alice stared at a point above Marie's head. "I think a further toast is in order" she said. "To Marie, *Sine qua non*." Once more, and without waiting for the others, her glass was drained.

"We all played our parts." Marie looked steadily back at Alice. She picked up the bottle and examined it before offering a further refill. "We're all 'implicated', as the police might say."

"The police won't be bothering us again," Alice said firmly. "And don't worry, I'm not talking about 'grassing' or whatever the word is. But you're the genius, Marie. Without you we couldn't have done it."

"It was your spotting him, you see, dear, that made it all possible," Pearl said, smiling admiringly. Her glass, still virtually full, was held between the palms of hands which, fingers extended, made her look as if she was at prayer. "When Alice phoned to tell me what was going on, you could have knocked me out with a duster."

Alice turned to her, her look one of ribald bemusement. "You *what?*"

"I'm trying to avoid the use of cliché." Pearl was blushing.

"Oh, of course," Marie said. "How are the classes going?"

"Quite well, I think," Pearl said, after considering the question. "Although I do find the village hall a mite draughty. But the young man who tutors us—apparently he's written a whole novel, though I'm not sure it's been published—is very keen for us to find our own voices. As long as we don't use cliché, that is."

"You'd be better off doing jam-making at the WI," Alice said, her voice thick with suppressed laughter and, possibly, sherry, although her cough suggested that phlegm, too, might be a problem. Then, having cleared her throat, to Marie she said, "We're all in this together, I quite agree, so don't worry on that score. All for one and one for all." Her laugh turned back into a cough, wet, brambly. "Sorry," she said, slapping her chest with the flat of a hand and setting the gold bands on her wrist glittering and jingling. "I can't seem to shake off this damned cold." She took some medicinal sherry, cleared her throat, and resumed. "I was about to add we can't really call ourselves the Three Musketeers, can we? We're not men. No knee breeches or codpieces, and, not being male, we have no swords to wave about."

A chesty laugh, another application of medicine, and she added, "Marie, to use a phrase Pearl would no doubt want us to avoid, it was your eagle eye that spotted him." She sighed. "It's as much as I can do to see across a room nowadays, let alone notice what's going on at roof-top level a whole street away."

Marie accepted the compliment, if compliment it was, with a wry shrug. "Though of course," she said, "what alerted me was the fact that *nothing* was going on. He was simply *there*. Standing, or perhaps I should say, *propped* against the lum, smoking a cigarette and looking about him." She gazed thoughtfully at Alice's empty glass but made no offer of a further refill. "That was what struck me as odd," she said, her eyes studying her own glass. "Making not so much as a pretence of work. The soul of idleness. In which case, I asked myself, why was he up there?"

"Quite." Pearl said, with some asperity, as Marie raised her eyes and looked at her, and Alice added her own, more wholehearted note of indignation. "Exactly. Why indeed?"

"But it was pure luck, and I don't deny it, that it was precisely the moment, the moment when he was standing on your roof, that I happened to be re-hanging the bedroom curtains."

"I really should give my curtains a good wash," Pearl said, sighing. "Even in the country they get grubby. Though not as quickly as they do in the city." And she raised the glass to her lips, cheeks reddening from the small ingestion of sherry or her unguarded revelation of domestic dereliction, or both.

Ignoring Pearl's remark, Alice said, "He'd have got away with it, that's for sure, if you hadn't seen him. Serendipity, I think they call it."

"Do they really?" Pearl asked, exchanging rue for a sharper tone. "I call it daylight robbery. Taking money for doing nothing."

"Taking a *lot* of money for doing nothing," Alice said. "A hundred pounds in my case."

"I wonder why he only charged me fifty?" Pearl looked from Alice to Marie, and back again.

"Perhaps he thought his luck was in. Fifty, first time. Double or quits next up," Marie said, but Alice disagreed.

"He was a canny one. Gave me to understand that as well as tiles having come loose, he could see that the guttering needed to be cleaned out. Clogged with autumn leaves, apparently. That was why I had to cough up a hundred." She made a *moue* of disgust. "And I fell for it, the more fool me." A pause. "Ah, well, there's no fool like an old fool."

"He said that autumn leaves were *my* problem," Pearl said, sounding as though she rather resented anyone else laying claim to clogged guttering. Having set her glass slowly down on the table, she sat back, dabbing at her lips with the balled handkerchief she drew from her cardigan sleeve. "I suppose he could see that the tiles on the bungalow were good as new."

"Whereas I live in a rather older house." Alice turned to look at Pearl, "which has its disadvantages." But her look, and even more her blatant sigh, said otherwise. Better a house with character than a featureless bungalow. She shifted her gaze to the frayed, grey woollen sweater that stretched taut across both bosom and stomach, flicked away an invisible crumb, then with a further sigh that verged on the theatrical added, "Since Bernard's death I rattle about like a pea in a pod; but I really don't think I could *bear* to live in a bung—anywhere else."

Glancing to see how Pearl took the implied rebuke, Marie said quickly, "There are pros and cons to all kinds of houses, aren't there? I sometimes wish I was nearer the village centre. But then I'd not have the fields to look out on from the back of the house."

"And from the front you can keep a look-out for crooks up ladders." Alice rolled the stem of her empty glass between thumb and first finger of her right hand. "A good job for us all you saw him. And damned good, Marie, if you'll pardon my language, that you had your wits about you. It was your phone call that put me right about Mr Criminal's little tricks." And she looked up, nodding as though in agreement with words that hadn't been spoken.

"It would have been even better if I'd been in time to prevent you from paying him."

"Oh, you did more than enough. Your call put me smack on the *qui vive*, I can tell you. Made me realise that I'd have to phone poor old Pearl here." She laid a hand on her friend's arm, the gesture implying both care and a certain complacency. "He had the goodness to inform me, if you please, that he'd been to her place first and that that was how he'd spotted what 'needed doing' to my roof, as he so kindly explained. Put two and two together and what have you got? I knew he must have winkled money out of her."

"Fifty pounds," Pearl repeated, "almost all I had in my purse."

"A mere half of what I shelled out." Alice sighed extravagantly. Her sense of grievance was, she implied, twice that of her friend's. "What was I *thinking* of. Ginger would have been appalled."

"I'm afraid he diddled the two of us, hook, line and er…" Pearl stopped.

"Sinker," Alice said, "you may as well call a spade a spade, no point in beating about the bush. Why pussyfoot around perfectly good sayings?" And her laugh, tinged with genial contempt, brought on another brief fit of coughing.

"Anyway," Pearl said, concentrating on Marie, while Alice pushed up her spectacles in order to fist water from her eyes, "we made up for our mistake, didn't we?"

"Didn't we just," Alice said, recovering from her cough, and her smile, at first cautious, steadily expanded to one of girlish glee.

As though agreeing with this assessment, Marie said, relenting, "Shall we have some more sherry, I think we deserve it?"

But leaning across the table to fill the glass Alice held out to her, she suddenly stopped, said ruminatively, "I wonder whether he has—had—a wife."

"If so," Alice said, in a no-nonsense way, gesturing to Marie to continue, "she's a widow now. Like all of us," she added. Settling back into the sofa, her glass refilled, she gobbled down some sherry. "Perhaps that's what we should call ourselves. The

Three Merry Widows." But seeing the downturn of Marie's mouth, "Well, we'll think of something."

For a few moments there was silence as the three, concentrating perhaps on the task Alice had set them, once more raised glasses to their lips.

Eventually, Marie spoke. "Do we have to?" The question invited no reply.

And at the same time Pearl, who had taken a bird's sip of her sherry, said, "You know, when I saw him lying flat on the ground I thought for one dreadful moment he might still be alive."

Marie looked sharply enough at her guest, but said nothing.

Pearl coloured, blinked, gazed down at her feet.

"Hardly likely," Alice finally said, as though to herself. Turning to Pearl, she added severely, "*Anyone* could see that he'd broken his neck." A pause. "It was obvious. To *me*, anyway, and ...." Turning back to Marie, she said, with what might have been a suppressed giggle, "and dead men tell no tales."

Marie, speaking over those last words, said rapidly, "Although the plan was to teach him a lesson. It wasn't any more than that."

The other two were looking at her now, attentive, questioning, even dubious.

She spoke again, and this time her words were more carefully measured. "But when he stood on my doorstep repeating the rigmarole he'd given you, I was at first so angry I was lost for words. Furious, that's how I felt, absolutely furious." She stared past the couple seated opposite her on the sofa, remembering. "I think it was the smarmy grin on his face, and knowing that he'd got your money stowed in his pocket. You should have *seen* the way he looked. Taking for granted that he could make an idiot out of me. Out of *us*. Three old women."

She drained her sherry in one gulp, then stared at her hand as though willing it to lose the trembling that had also invaded her voice.

Watching her, eyebrow raised in speculative wonder, Alice said, "Well, Marie, I admire you. I don't think I could have thought that fast on *my* feet."

"No, indeed," Pearl said, her prompt agreement with Alice's words drawing a sharp look from the woman sitting beside her. But Pearl intended no slight. "It's quite wonderful how you managed to come up with such a plan," she said innocently.

"Quite so," Alice said.

"Oh," Marie's shrug was one of self-deprecating candour, "I couldn't have managed on my own, you know. Anyway," and she paused, smiled at her two guests, "I like being able to offer my friends tea once in a while." Rotating the sherry glass between thumb and index finger, she said, "Tea and cake. Followed by sherry. No more than you deserve. I called and you came. I regard that as true friendship."

But a second later, as though dismissing the matter, she said, reflectively, "Can you believe, these glasses were a wedding present from Gerald's sister. Fifty five years, they've lasted. Longer than Gerald." Her laugh, when it came, was without regret.

The others, who knew of her husband's lonely death in exile after Marie had chanced on evidence of his long-abandoned affair with a secretary, kept silent. Implacable, Alice had been known to call her friend, though never to Marie's face.

Now, she said, "The ambulance men were on the scene in a jiffy, I will say that for them." She swivelled her heavy body to watch as Marie, having stood, went to snap on the overhead lights before moving across to the window.

Leaning against the glass, Marie peered up and down the close before, with a sudden jerk of her wrist, she released the white blind which came clattering down against the darkening sky.

As she returned to her seat, she said, "After all, we couldn't leave him lying there, could we."

"Out of the question," Alice said.

And Pearl said, "The first-aid people presumably called the police?"

"I think we probably did that," Marie said. "When you phone emergency you can ask for more than one service, you know."

"I seem to remember that you did," Alice said. Then, to Pearl, she explained, her voice hinting at something near awe, "I couldn't have uttered a word, but Marie knew exactly what to say, *and* how to say it."

During the quiet which followed, broken only by the low rumble of an aeroplane heading toward the local airport, the three of them looked from floor to ceiling, then from one to one to the other, then back to the floor.

Finally, Alice said, "I saw the police go through his pockets. Once the ambulance men confirmed he was dead, that is."

"I expect they were looking for means of identification." Pearl's voice was no more than a murmur.

There was another pause.

"And then he was carted away in the ambulance," Marie said. "A shame, that." Her look challenged the others to agree with her.

Alice frowned in puzzlement. "What else could they do?"

"Oh, I don't mean they did anything *wrong*. I'm sure it was all very proper. There has to be a post mortem before the body can be removed for burial. The police explained that to me." She paused. "But your money went with him, is what I mean."

"Ah." Looking down at her glass, nestling between hands that rested on her pleated skirt, Pearl smiled modestly .

Alice swivelled to look enquiringly at her friend. "Pearl," she said, "what do you mean, 'Ah?' You have something to tell us. I can feel it in my bones."

And when Pearl did nothing but smile at her, Alice added, "On anyone else's face I would call that look downright duplicitous. Now, out with it."

Blushing with what had to be pleasure at her own resource, Pearl said, "I mean the money *didn't* go with him."

She looked defiantly at Alice, then, turning to Marie, said, her face now candid with pleasure, "While you two were inside phoning, I went through his pockets."

"You *what?*" Marie asked, and Alice said, "I *knew* she was up to something. Still waters and all that, if you'll forgive the cliché," and, winking at Marie, she slapped the pleated thigh beside her. "Attagirl," she said.

Pearl reached inside the blouse almost hidden under her cardigan and her two friends watched in wondering silence as she drew out a number of banknotes. "I rather think there may be more than a hundred and fifty pounds here," she said, bending over the notes which she was smoothing down as they lay in her lap.

"Good lord," Alice said, shaking her head in bluff wonderment. "I'd never have believed it." Her laugh of exultant relief brought on a violent coughing fit. When it was over, she said, once more lifting her glasses to scrub at her eyes, "Jolly well done, Pearl."

And as though to confirm Alice's estimate of their friend's achievement, Marie said, "We may as well finish the bottle."

"Push out the ferry," Pearl said, looking up from the notes she was counting, and frankly giggling. She nudged Alice. "To rhyme with sherry."

"You can't push a ferry," Alice said, demeanour recovered, her voice once more expressive of sturdy common sense, even superior wisdom.

"Oh, I don't know," Marie said. "We've pushed trickier things."

Which made them all laugh.

In the Sweat of Thy Face

I

Tear-Arse. Behind his back, that is. It was Joe to his face. Not that he was often spoken to, and when he himself spoke it was usually to give an order. You couldn't imagine falling into a conversation with him. It wasn't so much that he was unfriendly as that he gave no sign of expecting familiarity with or from the men who worked alongside him and whom he addressed in a thick, guttural voice as though his tongue was a size too large for his mouth and he found speaking difficult. Tear-Arse Joe. A man of few words.

At various times, and especially in the past few weeks, I've found myself trying to picture his face, Joe's face, but I'm not sure I can. Certain features, yes. He was clean shaven and had slightly swarthy skin, I remember, plus the fact that he was stockily built and not especially tall, may even have been on the short side. But that, and the blue overalls he always wore, is about it. Short back and sides? Yes, but then in the mid nineteen-fifties every working man paid a fortnightly visit to the barber's. Same for men in suits. The only "long-hairs" were artists and classical musicians. Nose? Eyes? Cheekbones? Nothing remarkable about any of them. No distinguishing features, you could say.

Except for his name. I don't mean his surname, which I learnt only after he'd finished at the factory. I mean the name he was known by, Tear-Arse,—his moniker as the term then was—and of which, for all I know, he was unaware. The first time I heard it spoken was with a mixture of awe and commiseration. "Blimey, you've got *him*. Tear-Arse. Bad luck." The words were spoken by a school-mate, Tony Bellerby, and they came back to me when I heard of Bellerby's recent death from a friend of those days, someone with whom I've kept in touch over the years. He phoned to tell me the news, wondered whether I might be going to the funeral. Probably not, I said. After all, once we'd left school and gone our separate ways Bellerby and I never again met, though from time to time I saw his name attached to reports and features in a succession of daily newspapers, and hadn't he for some years chaired a radio chat show? That was him, my friend said. That was the Tony Bellerby we'd known in our teenage years. Well, where was the funeral to be held? I was given the name of a town in Cornwall, together with the funeral date. Relieved to have a genuine excuse for non-attendance, I said that on that particular day I'd be in Manchester, talking to a library group.

"You're not about to retire, then?"

"Writers don't retire," I said.

The next day I sent a card of condolence to the address my friend had spelled out over the phone—Bellerby had a wife still living, his third, so I was informed,—and then, having done the needful, I forgot all about him and his funeral.

But on the train up to Manchester I suddenly heard Bellerby's voice, as distinct as if he, not the young woman who sat opposite me yattering into her mobile, had spoken. "Blimey, you've got *him*. Tear-Arse. Bad luck."

II

Summer 1954. Six weeks off from school. Half-a-dozen of us, class-mates, had applied for work at the local lino factory. "Casual labour" it was called, though as we soon found there was nothing casual about the work we were made to put in. The factory is long gone now—I read somewhere that it was closed down partly because of falling orders but also because the small, southern town where it stood finally decided its citizens could do without the appalling stink that crawled out of the factory's chimney and blanketed the town's streets—but memories of that time persist. Four sweaty, exhausting weeks I spent there, on night-shifts that lasted from six pm to six o'clock the following morning. Cut and blistered fingers, bruised upper arms, shoulders and neck that throbbed with the sheer aching fatigue of manoeuvring onto our gang's flat-bed trolley those endless rolls of lino, none less than six-feet high and weighing at least two-hundred pounds, sometimes far more, legs and back thrilling with the muscle-pain that came of half-carrying, half-pushing the rolls from out the shed where the lino was manufactured, then cut and trimmed, and transferring them to the upper floors of the warehouse (the ground floor was reserved for offices and canteen) or, reversing the process in fulfilment of orders received, loading the trolley and moving the lino rolls from warehouse down to the lorries that waited to take them to destinations across England. Then, as soon as you'd emptied the trolley's contents onto the lorries, it was back to the shed to collect further rolls for warehousing.

And all the time you'd be breathing in the rubbery, chemical reek that pervaded every corner of the factory, a reek that layered your tongue, clogged your throat and lungs, attaching itself to your clothes and your body, and which never seemed to wash off, even after repeated latherings and scrubbings in that pink, industrial, sandpaper-textured soap the factory supplied for the wash-house where we were meant to clean ourselves down at the end of each twelve-hour shift, though I was usually too tired to bother. I simply got on my bike, cycled home, and, wrapped in the immovable stink of chemicalised rubber, collapsed into bed.

I worked at the factory from mid-July to mid-August, by which time I'd earned enough money to take myself on a brief holiday and still have some cash left over, quite a bit, in fact. Then it was early September and time for me to return for a final year of school, most of the cuts healed, thighs and forearms by and large clear of bruises. They—the bruises—came from trying to intercept toppling rolls of lino. It was all too easy to knock against a roll, a sight harder to prevent it toppling. If *that* happened—and it frequently did—an entire row of the damned things would keel over, and then we'd have to lift them back into position. Sounds easy? Try it. No, it was far better to use thighs, arms, even your back, as props to steady an about-to-fall roll of heavy-duty lino. Hence, the bruises.

As I say, by the time I was back in school all but the most severe of these had faded. But not my memories of the work itself. And certainly not my memory of Tear-Arse.

III

If only I'd started work a day earlier I'd have avoided being one of his gangers. But having eaten a more than dodgy pork pie on Sunday I had to call in sick on Monday afternoon, and by Tuesday evening, when I reported for duty, the half-dozen gangs of four men and a leader had been assigned. All except Tear-Arse's. He got the ones who'd not been lucky enough to join another gang. Tear-Arse got the misfits, the newcomers, ones who'd been off ill or were simply elbowed out in the process of selection. I don't think he cared. He may not even have noticed. To repeat, Tear-Arse wasn't one for banter, let alone conversation. He was there to work, and the less talk there was the more work could be done. Other gangs chatted, even sang among themselves as they worked. Our gang, as I soon discovered, worked in virtual silence.

At the outset of each shift we lined up on the ground floor of the factory's warehouse, outside the washrooms. Gang leaders were handed a list of "dues" by the night manager, a short, sallow-complexioned man in a saggy grey suit and brylcreemed hair, who made his way across to us from his office at the far side of the building where you could hear typewriters hammering away and the occasional jangle of a telephone. *Mister* Carter, he made sure he was called, and he always had a cigarette dangling from the far left side of his mouth while he doled out the lists without much by way of comment. When he'd finished he'd say round his cigarette "Right, lads, let's make sure all these are taken care of before the end of the night," and then, with a dismissive nod of the head, he'd be gone. Behind his turned back men made V signs or more obscene gestures. Carter was not popular.

As for "dues," they were the rolls of lino awaiting dispatch. There were always hundreds of these orders to be met, and they were supposed to be evenly split between the six gangs. But in fact Tear-Arse's gang got more than its fair share. "Here you are, Joe, this is your little lot." The smile that went with Carter's words was a villainous smirk.

As soon as the lists were handed out, you set to work. This entailed taking the stairs two floors up to the higher warehouse floor—the one beneath which held off-cuts and reject rolls we didn't handle—where you collected a flat-bed trolley, about six feet by four, then located the rolls needed to complete one "due." You heaved each roll onto the trolley, ten or twelve of them to a load, looking like a consignment of tree-trunks and weighing about the same. You then got ready to push the trolley, two each side with the leader in front grasping the iron-shafted handle, and between you steered it into a vast, open-front lift from where you descended to the loading bay and, lastly, lifted the rolls onto lorries waiting to trundle across the country to wherever the lino was needed.

From all I could tell, the need was nation-wide. In those post-war years, linoleum, or lino as everyone called it, was in such huge demand that our factory was hard put to supply all the orders it received. Hence the twelve-hour night shifts, and even with six gangs working throughout the night some "dues" would be left over for the day shift.

The work was ceaseless. You loaded your trolley, took it down, unloaded, and then you guided the now empty trolley across to the "making" shed where newly-prepared rolls of lino were waiting to be taken up to the warehouse floor. And before you collected another "due" you had to off-load the newly-finished rolls and stack them upright in rows according to pattern and length. Six-foot reds here, five-foot blue with roses there, even eight feet—often pretend parquet—in another long row. The rows were meant to be separated from each other by metal barriers, but some of these barriers were missing, others were too flimsy to hold back an entire row of lino rolls that would in all likelihood come crashing down if one was accidentally dislodged. And, as I've said, if *that* happened, you had to heft each of the damned things back upright.

Injuries? Of course there were, some serious. Broken limbs, the occasional amputation. Deaths, too. It was rumoured that one couple, who'd sneaked into a far corner of the warehouse for a quickie, were crushed under a toppling row of six-foot greens intended for a newly-built hospital up north. "Might as well load the bodies on," some cold-hearted sod was supposed to have remarked. "There'll be a sawbones to use the parts in A and E."

To say the work was back-breaking isn't mere cliché. Quite a few of those who worked as gangers at the factory ended up with a stoop and a limp. You'd see a few of the worst cases shuffling along the town's streets. It was a bit like the "bends" from which sponge divers used to suffer. The constant heavy lifting was bad enough. What made it worse was that, once you were on a shift, and leaving aside breaks of quarter-of-an-hour at 9pm, and another six hours later, plus half-an-hour for a canteen meal at midnight, you never stopped.

Well, we, Tear-Arse's gang, never stopped. Other gangs were cannier. They found ways of taking breathers between fulfilling each "due", and as a result they finished the shift tired but, as it were, still standing. Tony Bellerby, in common with the others of my school mates who'd signed on for a month, was one of a gang whose leader took good care to complete his list of "dues" just as the six o'clock bell rang for the end of night-shift. Tony told me about that when we stopped for a tea-break my first night at the factory.

"Who's your gang-leader?" he asked.

"Someone called Joe," I said. "I don't know his surname."

And that was when he said the words that came back to me on the train up to Manchester. "Blimey. You've got *him*. Tear-Arse. Bad luck."

I sat with Tony again, this time at midnight dinner-break a few days after I'd begun work at the factory. "What's it like?" he asked.

"Knackering," I told him.

"That's why he's called Tear-Arse." And Tony, grinning, told me that his father had heard from a drinking pal who'd worked for a while at the factory that Joe was a man to avoid at all costs. He wasn't a slave driver, "because he drives himself as hard as he drives his gang," but, Tony said, there was something a bit mad, or so it seemed, about his silent intensity, his determination never to cease from work which, face it, couldn't by any stretch of the imagination be thought of as fulfilling. It was simply hard graft.

There were rumours, Tony said, that Tear-Arse had gypsy blood in him. Hence, his slightly swarthy skin, his voice, a strange, guttural way of speaking as though English wasn't his native tongue. And then there was his name. Joe. A well-known gypsy name, so Tony told me.

Maybe, I said, but added something along the lines that I'd never heard there was a proven connection between being a Romany and a life of endless toil.

Changing tack, Tony agreed. He also told me that speaking for himself he rather fancied life on the open road, anything rather than being cooped up in a factory or office all day long. Well, we were young.

And now Bellerby was dead. Hadn't he at one time been called, or dubbed himself, a roving reporter? Perhaps at least part of his wish had come true. If so, good for him. But in the summer of 1954 I was more bothered about the twelve-hour shifts that for me, at least, were temporary, whereas for the men who worked there permanently what they did seemed less a job than a life-sentence. I said as much to Bellerby, because I remember he came back with "Not if you know how to pace yourself," or words to that effect, and he went on to ask me how I got on with the three other members of Tear-Arse's gang. Apart from their names, I didn't know much about any of them, I told him, though I was pretty sure that at least two, Mick and Don, they were called, wanted to transfer to other gangs. The third, Albie, seemed more ready to accept Tear-Arse. Or maybe he simply put up with him. Anything for a quiet life. Which you certainly got because, I added, the four of us never had time to talk. The pace was non-stop frenetic. Why? There was nothing to be gained by working as Tear-Arse did because, far from being able to knock off early, the only result of handing in your completed list of "dues" was that Carter produced a few extras, just for you. Well, thanks.

Did we get more money for our efforts? Did we hell. All gangers were on flat wages, paid out at the end of each week. Once you'd finished your last shift and after you'd done your best to wash and brush up, each gang presented itself (ours last, naturally) at the hatch where wages were paid out—a hole in the wall beside the manager's office. A brown envelope with your name written on it would be pushed over the sill by Sally, the Wages Clerk—known to one and all as Our Gal Sal—you'd sign for it, then stand aside while you ripped open the envelope and checked to see you'd been paid what you were owed. "All present and correct" someone would say, another voice would add, "Yeh, sod it, no extras."

That was Albie, the one ganger in our crew I talked to, or, more to the point, the one who talked to me. The other two, Mick and Don, barely opened their mouths. I could tell they didn't much care for what Tear-Arse put them through, but they went about their work with a kind of stoic resentment. As for Sal, she was a neighbour of Albie's, so he informed me the first time I picked up my wages. "Need to keep my nose clean when she's around," he said, cheerfully, "don't want her telling tales over the garden fence."

At the start of my second week at the factory I asked Albie, as we stood in the tea-break queue, if Tear-Arse was paid extra for being the management's blue-eyed boy. But no. Our Gal Sal had let Albie know that Joe took home the same as the rest of us. No perks, no back-handers. "There's one born every minute," was a saying of that time, and from the smug look on Carter's face when he came out from his office to thank us as we accepted our money you could tell that was exactly what he was thinking. So were other gangers who, whenever they saw us as we raced past with our loaded trolley, would shake their heads in mock wonderment or, even, treat us to a few notes of "Whistle While You Work".

If Joe noticed any of this response, some of it no more than genial contempt, he certainly didn't let it disturb him. He was impervious to any of it. And unlike the rest—I mean the rest of the gangers, *all* of them—he never seemed to work up a sweat, even though he always wore a tie under the collar of his dark-blue shirt, and, again unlike the rest of us, kept the sleeves of that shirt buttoned to the wrist. Beneath his blue overalls he seemed impeccably dressed, as neat and tidy at the end of a twelve-hour shift as at the beginning. Impervious, imperturbable, and impeccable. And a hard task-master. That was Joe.

He was also a loner. He never came into the canteen, preferring to take his breaks on his own, hunched over the trolley, packet of sandwiches and thermos pulled from the small haversack he brought to work each night and which he hung on his peg—Tear-Arse's peg—in the washroom, along with his donkey jacket and a black leather cap.

IV

But then one shift, a Friday evening at the beginning of August and the end of my third week, he arrived without his haversack. "Wife gone away," he said in that strange, guttural voice, hanging up his cap and turning to me as, early for once, I hung up my own jacket. The information was given as though reluctantly and at once he turned away and marched to the lift that would take us up to work.

Well, well. So Joe was married! This would come as news to others who had from time to time speculated about his private life and concluded that he had none. Speculation was all it could be. As we made our way back to work after a canteen break, the four in our gang might exchange a few words about films or music, but the waiting gang-leader, ready for action, refused to be drawn into our conversations. All we got from him was a barked command, a thick, accented statement, "Work is waiting," and off we went.

He seemed to have no interest in the world beyond the lino factory. Once, one of the older men in our gang, trying to be friendly, asked him as we went down in the lift if he supported any football team, Joe's only response was to shake his head.

What about films? Had he seen *Shane?* Another shake of the head. Music? The Ted Heath Orchestra would be playing a concert that coming Saturday at a nearby ballroom and there was a clamour for tickets. Albie could get Joe one if he liked. The look Joe directed at his questioner suggested a kind of baffled incomprehension. "Music?" he said, and, intending either an explanation for his own indifference or his opinion of Ted Heath, he added, "not music."

After that, the four of us more or less gave up. We took his orders and, when we could, we talked among ourselves, a little. But even when, wages pocketed as we sauntered to the bike sheds exchanging information about how we planned to lash out on entertainment for the coming evening—the flicks, a visit to the dog-track, dancing at the local Mecca—even then, Joe, who was with us because, like the rest, he had a bike to collect, said nothing, simply retrieved his machine from its usual place, checked the tyre pressure, mounted, briefly waved, and rode off into the early morning air.

Watching him as he cycled away one Saturday morning, Mick asked, "What do you reckon old Tear-Arse does over the weekend?"

There was silence. Then Don said, "Probably goes straight to bed and don't get up until Monday evening. Lies there dreaming of work."

Only Albie said, gnomically, "He's alright, Tear-Arse is."

V

That Friday night when Joe let slip the news about his wife, I was looking forward to sharing his cloakroom revelation with the others. But I couldn't. Because, bereft of his thermos and packet of sandwiches, he chose for once to sit with the rest of us during our breaks and though he said nothing his silence inhibited our own chatter. When we entered the canteen at tea-break, Tear-Arse leading the way, there was a certain amount of ironic applause, of which he took no notice, but some moments before we needed to leave he was up on his feet and we followed him out to looks of commiseration from the other gangs.

Same at dinner. We bent in near silence over plates of sausage, beans and chips. It was pretty damned depressing, especially given that all around us other factory workers, including the gangers, were making plenty of noise, though at odd moments I'd notice someone or other look across at our table, and, if not in Joe's eye-line, grimace sympathetically at us. One of them, a man I'd heard muttering in the washroom about gyppo Joe, even cupped a hand to his ear and leant in the direction of our table, in mocking recognition of the silence in which we sat.

But then Mick said something about how, with the weekend coming up, and a family wedding in store, he planned to get "rat-arsed."

I'd been reading Oscar Wilde. "Work," I said to the table in general, "is the curse of the drinking classes."

They nodded and began to laugh. "Dead right," Don said. But Joe, lifting his head, stared from me to the others and we were no longer laughing. He spoke into the silence. And for once he spoke an entire sentence. "Work" he said, "is the condition of man."

The words fell like a dead weight between us. Had anyone else spoken them you could have imagined he was being ironic or, perhaps, and assuming he wasn't raving mad, was hoping to start an argument, just for the hell of it. But not Joe. The sentence, brief as it was, uttered in that peculiar guttural voice of his, seemed forced out of him. It wasn't directed at me, though I would have been the one to reprove. But no, although his words were audible enough, he spoke them as if to himself, as if reminding himself of a truth he was in danger of forgetting, and having uttered the sentence he lowered his gaze while the rest of us stared from one to the other in a kind of stupefied perplexity, too stunned to speak. Only Albie, I saw, looked as though he might want to say something. He lifted his head from where he had been staring into his tea mug, and as he did so began to open his mouth, but then, with an almost imperceptible shrug, he closed it again. He had though, risked a look at Tear-Arse, a look that might just have been one of wry assent. Then he went back to staring into his mug.

A couple of years later, when I read *Little Dorrit* and came to Pancks's words about work, I remembered that moment in the lino factory. I was a university student then, and I read Dickens under plain brown covers, as it were, because he wasn't a novelist we were supposed to admire. A then-famous critic called F.R. Leavis had announced that, *Hard Times* apart, "there is nothing for the mature mind" in Dickens, with the result that most university students and their lecturers made a practice of curling the lip at the mere mention of his name.

By the time I opened *Little Dorrit* I'd read enough of Dickens's novels to realise there wasn't anything for the mature mind in Leavis's ridiculous pronouncement. *Little Dorrit* strengthened that conviction. Pancks is a man who, so he himself says, is made only for work. "Rattle me out of bed early, set me going, give me as short a time as possible to bolt my meals in, and keep me at it. Keep me always at it, and I'll keep you always at it, you keep somebody else always at it." For Pancks, men are made for work.

And reading Pancks's sardonic account of what he calls being kept "always at it" because it—work—is "the Whole Duty of Man in a commercial country," I inevitably thought back to Tear-Arse. By then I knew more about him than I ever did when I worked at the lino factory, and recalling his utterance I had to wonder whether he shared Pancks's bitter understanding of "Duty."

"Work is the condition of man." None of us sitting round that canteen table on a Friday night in 1954 was able to answer back. We were simply too amazed—*awed* might be the better word—to open our mouths. The words seemed to have been scooped from some primal place, as if he, Tear-Arse, was the mouthpiece, no more, no less, through which a dark, comfortless spirit found utterance.

For a moment I did, I know, wonder whether to ask him what he meant by "condition." I even thought of quoting a line of Milton I'd come across in my A Level reading. "Wilt thou enjoy the good, then cavil the conditions". Milton, I'd been told, used the word to mean a provisionally granted status. What's good comes with conditions attached. If Joe was using the word in that sense then we were off the hook, weren't we? Working at the lino factory, all that back-breaking, monotonous pulling and heaving, could hardly be thought of as enjoying the good.

But a glance at Joe's set face was enough to put a stop to my words. Besides, the others, Mick, Don and Albie—especially

Albie—wouldn't have been impressed. I could imagine how they'd react. Better a Tear-Arse than a smart arse.

So I kept quiet, and after a moment or two Joe, having taken care to adjust his shirt cuffs, stood up from the table and in silence we followed him out of the canteen. As we pushed through the swing doors someone made the noise of a sheep. Baa-aa. Joe didn't pause. Straight-backed, he led the way back to our waiting trolley. It was as if he was anxious to prove the truth of his words.

VI

And yet when we reported for work the following Monday evening, the beginning of my last week, Joe wasn't there. An unfamiliar gang-leader was standing by our trolley, examining the "dues" list, while Mick, Don and Albie, sprawled across the trolley, grinning, at their ease.

"Where's Joe?" I asked, surprised.

The gang-leader, glancing up from his list of "dues", shook his head as he looked me over. Then he held out his hand. "Graham," he said.

I told him my name, then looked from him to the others, waiting for an explanation. Was Graham filling in for a night? Perhaps Joe was off ill, though he'd seemed fine when we parted the previous Saturday morning. Besides, a man of that strength. You felt that indomitable will-power itself would have brought him to the factory.

But then another thought came. The words Joe had uttered in the cloakroom last Friday. *Wife gone away.* Might she be ill? Dead even? Or, it came to me, perhaps she'd vamoosed, simply run off. Was Joe's absence caused by some domestic crisis?

"Joe's finished," Albie said, "Asked for his cards. He'd have been given them anyway."

"*What?* You mean Joe's been sacked?"

And when the others nodded in confirmation, I said, "But why? What's he done?"

The man called Graham said tersely, "Lucky they didn't set the law on him."

More bewildering still. Had Joe been filching…goods or money? But that didn't seem likely. Even if he'd wanted to he couldn't have smuggled a roll of lino out of the factory, and Tear-Arse simply wasn't the kind of man to go looking for stray cash or fingering anyone's wallet.

Graham said, "I'm sorry to say that your late workmate offered physical violence to the manager, Reg Carter." Then, dropping the pompous tone, he added, "Knocked the poor sod spark out. Broke his jaw. The way Reg hit the deck I'm told it could have been a nasty case of concussion." He paused. "Or worse," he said. "Could have killed him."

I suppose my surprise—no, disbelief—must have registered with them all, because Don said, "It's the truth, kiddo. Want to send Carter a bunch of flowers?" And he and Mick laughed.

I looked at Graham. "But *why*? And when? I mean, when did this happen?" And before he could reply, I said, appealing to Albie and the other two gangers, "We all left together last Saturday morning. Didn't we?"

They were propped on their elbows now, gazing up at me from the trolley, two of them at least enjoying my bewilderment.

"But then he came back in," Albie said, who wasn't laughing. "And belted Carter."

"You mean he returned in order to hit him? But *why?* He must have had a reason. Has Carter explained?"

"Carter can't speak. His jaw's wired up, and he's in hospital, under observation."

"What, *police* observation?"

Graham shook his head. "As I told you, the law is not involved." He was back to pompous mode. "We have the firm's name to consider. Its reputation."

Behind him, I saw Albie raise a sardonic eyebrow. Graham, the bosses' man.

And meanwhile, the bosses' man was explaining to me that the doctors had no alternative but to keep Reg Carter in hospital until they could be certain there was no delayed concussion. "They're hopeful he'll be out by the middle of the week, though he won't be back here for a while, not until his jaw's mended."

"But if Joe did that much damage surely the police ought to be involved?"

Graham again shook his head, this time vehemently. There was clearly something about the incident I didn't understand.

"Would anyone like to explain to me?" I asked.

"OK." Albie, serious now, was sitting upright. "Carter asked for it," he said, looking in turn at the other two gangers, who half nodded, though I noticed Graham stared, blank faced, at Albie. Was he warning him not to say too much. If so, it seemed to have little effect.

"Joe didn't come back in *intending* to belt Carter," Albie told me, "All he did was ask if he could transfer to the day shift for a week. No idea why, unless he couldn't stand the sight of us lot. That's a joke, by the way."

I said, "It may be something to do with his wife. That could explain why he didn't want to say anything in front of us. He waited until we were off the premises and then nipped back in."

And when Albie and the others stared enquiringly at me I repeated to them Joe's three-word revelation of the previous Friday.

"What did he mean, do you reckon? Did he tell you any more?" The way Albie asked the question strengthened my feeling that he felt more sympathetic than the rest of us to our former gang-leader.

"No idea," I told him. "She's ill? She's left him?"

"Or," Mick said, "with her away, there's someone or something at home he needs to look after of an evening."

"Unlikely," I said. "And it still doesn't explain why he floored Carter."

"OK," Albie said again. "This is what I know, and what I know is pretty well kosher given that I got it from Our Gal Sal. She was round to see me and the wife Saturday lunchtime. According to her," he said, speaking as though he was making a statement, "Carter was passing the time of day with her as they got ready to leave the factory, probably throwing her a chat-up line. Then Tear-Arse appears. Come to request shifting from nights to days."

"And?"

"And Carter asked him why. Sal said Tear-Arse muttered something about a change being as good as a rest and Carter said that wasn't much of a reason but he'd see what he could do. He'd let him know on Monday evening. Tear-Arse said he'd appreciate that and turned to go. And that's when it happened, because Carter, reckoning that Joe had slung his hook, said something along the lines of these gyppos thinking they can swing the lead and that Tear-Arse wouldn't have tried that on with Adolf—she couldn't remember the exact words, but she did realise that Tear-Arse must have still been within hearing, because she saw him stiffen, turn, then he marched back, grabbed Carter by the shoulder, hauled him round and hit him with a haymaker that would have floored Marciano."

Albie paused. "Blood everywhere, Sal told us, soon as Carter's head hit the deck. And Tear-Arse staring down at him like a madman, as though he wanted to finish him off. But then he just shrugged, gave her a stare, and walked away."

I must have looked how I felt, astonished to the point of disbelief, because Albie said, "No word of a lie."

Mick and Don were looking at Albie and grinning. They'd already heard the gist of the tale, but they were enjoying it all over again. They might not much like Tear Arse, but they liked Carter a whole lot less.

As for me, I could scarcely credit Albie's words. "What happened then," I asked.

"And then," he said, "Sal must have screamed, because some of the half-day shift, who were just arriving, came running up, and before you could say knife an ambulance had been phoned for and Carter was on his way to hospital."

Having finished his story, Albie, levering himself off the trolley, stood, gave Graham a mock salute and said, "Right, guv, ready for duty." And to me, "And now you know as much as the rest of us."

"Least said, soonest mended," Graham said.

"Until Carter's jaw is mended he'll not be saying anything," Albie said. He looked steadily at me but I saw the ghost of a smile that flickered and was gone. "And I don't suppose he'll want to say much then."

"What makes you so sure?"

"Didn't you hear what Graham said?" He turned to our new gang-leader. "We don't want the factory's name dragged through mud, do we?"

There was an indefinable taunt about the way he spoke the words, and about the way, lip curled, he responded to Graham's silent nod.

"Better get to it," Graham said by way of changing the conversation. He flourished the list in the air. "There's a full set of orders here. Come on, now lads. Chop, chop."

With which awkward attempt at joviality he picked up the trolley handle and motioned for us to follow him to the lift. And that seemed to be that.

But later Albie, standing next to me in the tea-break queue, tapped me on the shoulder and, his voice low, said, "If you're still wondering why Joe nearly killed Carter, ask yourself why he always kept his shirt sleeves buttoned down."

I turned to him. "Not a clue," I said. "Why did he?"

"You really can't guess?"

I shook my head.

As though explaining something to a backward child, Albie said, "Maybe to hide the numbers tattooed on his arm?"

And then, and only then, I understood.

So I wasn't surprised by the note which, as we left the factory two mornings later, Albie handed me. He'd found it pinned to his coat in the cloakroom. Written in stiff uncials the note said simply, "WORK WILL MAKE YOU FREE!! You understand, I think. Good luck to you, Albie, and to the others. Joseph Solomon."

The First Time

Nothing can prepare you. Not words, not music, not paintings. People write poems to and about the "mighty waters, rolling ever more"; "The unplumbed, salt, estranging sea"; about how "The slopping of the sea grew still one night", composers try to capture its sounds—"Fingal's Cave", "La Mer", "Sea Symphony", "Peter Grimes"; artists paint it—Ruysdael, Gericault, Turner, Stanfield,—but words, music, and especially those stiff, starchy, immobilised waves on canvas, not excepting even Hokusai's watery, blue-lunged swirls—*nothing* can begin to convey the water's restless, swaying, muscled movements. Old salts will tell you about the sea's moods. But until you've actually *seen* it, watched the shifts from blue to malachite green, from sullen grey to black, you can't really understand. Moods? What do they mean? *Moods*? What does *the word* mean?

And then, the size, the fact that it fills not merely the eye but the mind, extends as far and as wide as you can see and that what's sprawling in front of you is only the beginning, the edge, the prelude.... That perhaps most of all. The sheer blue *immensity*.

I was eight when I caught my first glimpse of the sea. In the summer of 1945, with the war in Europe newly over and the conflict in the Far East about to end, my mother decided to take my sister and me on holiday. For a week we would leave behind the Midlands village where we'd spent most of the war years. We were off to Torquay.

Torquay. I vaguely confused the name with that of Turkey, perhaps because I'd seen a photograph of its esplanade featuring palm trees. Didn't such trees belong to the Levant? Besides, Torquay was, my mother said, a place of sun and sand. Peering at a photograph she showed me, I think I half-hoped to see camels among the palms, led by a swarthy-looking, moustachioed individual in a fez, his white-stockinged feet encased in curl-toed slippers. But the men caught by the camera as they strolled along Torquay's sea-front wore suits, their heads protected from the weather by trilbies, caps, the occasional bowler hat; and the women on their arms were in calf-length dresses and coats. Nothing exotic in that.

Still, I could dream. And while the photographed men and women I studied looked identical with ones I saw about Midland streets, at least Torquay had the sea.

We were going to Torquay. And, like the men in the song who joined the navy, we were going to see the sea.

Why Torquay? It was where my parents came from, it was where my father's parents lived, as they had done all their lives, and although because of wartime travel restrictions I'd never met either grandparent, I knew various things about Torquay beyond what the photograph showed me. I knew, for instance, that it was referred to as "The Queen of the English Riviera". It was favoured by occasional visits from royalty, and the sea around it was said to be warmed to an un-English tepidity by something called the Gulf Stream (which I vaguely imagined to be a river fed by hot-water pipes). I knew that it "boasted"—that odd word—several beaches, some pebbled, others sandy, all of them featuring rock-pools, and all of them backed by large, "posh" hotels, as well as grandly cultivated public gardens; I knew that the town, built on the side of a hill, was sheltered from northern winds by tall, red-clay cliffs.

How much of this my mother had told me and how much I'd picked up from hearsay and from a battered old book in blue cloth binding—*The History of Torquay*, it was called and the author, J.T. White, had apparently been a friend of my grandfather's—I can't possibly recall. But in the weeks during which she planned our railway journey and bought tickets with her Co-op savings— not stamps but thin pieces of tin, hexagon-shaped and about the size of a sheriff's star, each stamped with the sum of money it stood surety for, 1d, 3d, 6d—in those weeks I repeatedly took White's *History* out of the bookcase and stared at its illustrations of gardens, of hotels, some no bigger than large houses, others suggesting knightly castles; I studied the harbour with its yachts and crowded pleasure steamers—*Trips Round the Bay 1/6d*—and I looked long and hard at photographs of the sea beyond Torbay and Goodrington Sands, though I couldn't get out of my head the sepia images which suggested that the bay waters must themselves be toffee-coloured. If so, they were entirely different from the ocean I could see in my boy's version of *Robinson Crusoe*. The illustrations to this showed Crusoe's island surrounded by a sea creamily blue, although in one of the illustrations tall, green waves loomed above the beach where Crusoe knelt to inspect a footprint. Blue and green. I had no idea what the sea surrounding Crusoe's island was called but I did know that the toffee-coloured sea we would be heading for was called the English Channel, which made it sound narrow, a kind of ditch, gutter-like even. No wonder if the sea there should be brown.

But what then to make of the two water-colours that hung on the dining-room wall? "Thatcher Rock" and "Heather Rock", they were called, and, so my mother explained, showed two craggy outcrops jutting up from a blue sea just off Babbacombe, itself a village round the corner of the bay from Torquay, and the place where my now-dead maternal grandfather had been born. The grass-tufted rocks, viewed from slightly above, were circled by gulls, the water surrounding their bases was light blue, sunlit, frilly as lace cuffs, and, in the words of my friend, John Masters, about as exciting as a bowl of lard. "Besides," he said, "I bet the sea's more like that brown in the book you showed me. Mucky as a gutter."

John, who lived next door with his mother and gran, and whose father, like mine, was away in the army, hadn't seen the real thing any more than I had, but as we stood side by side and looked at the paintings, he announced that he couldn't understand why anyone should be keen to make the sea's acquaintance. "It's not like Sapcote Woods," he said.

I knew what he meant. You could get lost in the woods. You could spend hours playing hunters and settlers, cowboys and

Indians, you could climb trees in search of birds' eggs and when you tired of that you could drop down to reach into the chill water of the shallow stream that wandered through the woods and pull out clumps of watercress to chew on, as, socks shoved into pockets and shoes tied by their laces and hung round the neck, you paddled along the stream's stony bottom, trawling for minnows and sticklebacks; occasional sounds, a branch falling or a bird clattering up from cover, made it easy to believe that wild animals roamed among the trees, and when you'd had enough of the stream you could dry your feet and track the path that led to the gypsy encampment. There, hidden by undergrowth, you could watch women as they crouched about the fire in which, John told me, they baked hedgehogs rolled in clay.

What had the sea to offer by comparison with all that? Who needed the sea?

I must have put that question to my mother, though not in those words. She smiled. "Wait and see," she said, "that's what Mr Asquith always told people. Wait and see."

"And what will I see?"

"The sea, of course. And you and your sister will be stunned," she said. She paused. "And that's a promise," she added. "Stunned."

***

Not long ago, I was looking at an old picture book of Torquay I'd found on a second-hand bookstall. The inside cover told me that it had been published in 1910 and that it was issued on behalf of the Torbay Hoteliers' Association. Some of the photographs were familiar. Views of the Public Gardens, of the wide, groyned beaches, of the harbour. And there, studded with full-sailed yachts and, nearer to shore, the heads and shoulders of bathers, was the sea, reminding me exactly of the liquid caramel tint I'd encountered in White's *History* seventy years earlier. And as I looked I heard my mother's voice in my ear distinctly as if she was in the room. "*Stunned.*"

It had never occurred to me to think much about the word's meaning, but now my curiosity was piqued. As soon as I got home I took down the relevant volume of my Oxford English Dictionary. This is what I found: "stunned: that has been stunned; dazed; astounded, bewildered." Oddly, it seems to me, the initial letter is given in lower case, whereas "Stun", "Stunned", and "Stunning" all warrant upper case initials. As though there's something almost trivial, perhaps a bit shaming, about being stunned. (And no, I didn't look up "shaming.") But—dazed; astounded, bewildered. *Was* that right? *Was* that how it had been?

"You and your sister will be stunned."

For my eighth birthday someone, an aunt I think, had presented me with a novel about a boy who in the days of sailing ships ran away to sea. The boy meets with adventures remarkably similar to those I was familiar with from *Treasure Island*. There may well have been a pirate with a wooden leg and a talking parrot. Even at the age of eight I knew the novel was a cheap imitation and I didn't bother to read to the end. I did, though, return again and again to a colour illustration of the boy, whose name I can't remember, lying at length on a grassy knoll, propped up on his elbows, chin cupped in his hands as he stares out over what the illustration identified as the Bristol Channel.

A few years later, I came across the boy's simulacrum when I saw a colour reproduction of Millais's "The Boyhood of Raleigh". He's the one on the right, dressed in a suit of black velvet, listening to the tales spun by a Robinson Crusoe-looking salt who was, I learnt, a portrayal of that old rogue, Edward Trelawney, Byron's friend. In Millais's picture the boy is facing toward the viewer. In the original—which was how I thought of it, though of course it was the other way round—he is looking away. Beyond both is water, blue, splashed with white. Not caramel, but otherwise the same undifferentiated, uninteresting sea.

Stunned? By *that*? No, but still....

***

We travelled by coach from Hinckley to Leicester, at Leicester we took a stopping train to Birmingham, and then, at Birmingham, assisted by a porter who agreed to help my mother locate the seats she'd reserved, we clambered onto the already crowded express that would eventually deliver us to Torquay.

My mother and sister sat side by side, backs to the engine, I was in the window seat facing them for the journey. It was by far the longest my sister and I had ever been on. Stations came and went. Cheltenham, Gloucester, Bristol. All windows were open but the heat was oppressive, there was an acrid smell of sweating bodies, the fug of tobacco smoke, a scratchy, uncomfortable feeling of carriage-cloth against my arms and legs. "Don't fidget", my mother said from time to time. "Read your books." But I noticed that she regularly lowered the library book she had brought with her, preferring to gaze out at the fields and red-brick villages we were clattering past.

"Who *is* Rumer Godden?" I asked her. "A man or a woman?" Rumer Godden was the name of the author printed on the dust-jacket.

"What do you think?" my mother asked me.

"A man?"

"A camel," my sister said, and giggled, kicking me under the table as she did so.

I kicked her back and she stuck her tongue out at me.

It was that kind of a journey.

***

At Taunton, which, according to the station clock, we reached at a quarter past one, my mother unwrapped the sandwiches she'd prepared before we left home. "Exeter next," she said as she uncorked lemonade for us children and poured herself tea from her thermos.

"Where's Exeter?" we asked. "Is it near where we're going?"

Exeter, my mother told us, was the county town of Devon. "And then—the sea."

"How will we know when we see it?" my sister asked.

"Is that seat taken, duck?"

My mother told me to move my book and the woman who had asked sat heavily down beside me. She was wearing a dark blue dress and black straw hat. Was she some kind of a nurse?

She looked across at my sister and my mother, both dressed in what our mother called "Sunday best"—a rarely worn pleated, grey skirt and white blouse with maroon jacket for her, my sister in a green-and-white striped dress that had been jointly made by our mother and the woman next door, whose sewing machine my mother had borrowed.

"Going anywhere nice?" the woman asked. She had a deep, rumbling voice.

"Torquay," I said.

"Ah, well, you'll want to look your best for that, I reckon." But she was still looking across at my sister and mother. "Don't want to get smutches on yer new clothes."

I knew what she meant. Women were expected to sit with backs to the engine so that flakes of soot drifting through open windows wouldn't settle on them. Whenever on our long journey south we thundered into a tunnel someone would close the nearest window and hot, ashy smells filled the carriage, so that it came as a relief to be once more out into the light, windows prised apart to let in a rush of air.

"I'll not be going far as Torquay," the woman said as we emerged from one especially long period of blackness during which we all sat staring at our unsmiling reflections in window glass. "Near as, though."

And when my mother enquired politely where she'd be leaving the train, the woman said "Newton Abbot, duck. I'm seeing my sister for the day."

Which explained why she hadn't any luggage with her apart from the large handbag she was hugging to her stomach.

My sister, whose question hadn't been answered, repeated it. "How will we know when we see the sea?" Chanting the words now, she repeated them once more. "See the sea."

"See the sea?" The woman laughed. Reaching across to pat the girl on the cheek, "You'll know right enough, duck," she said.

The train was slowing now as it ran through fields and beside a curve of river; there were sidings, engine sheds painted cream and brown and, then, at a long, crowded platform, we jerked to a halt, brakes screeching. To the accompaniment of a great hiss of steam that died away in a series of panting sounds, women and children—there were hardly any men—shouldered their way into our carriage. Those who couldn't find seats filled the central aisle, some carrying wicker baskets, others gripping leather bags stuffed with towels, patched footballs, the wooden handles of small spades, cricket bats, and, uniquely, a wood-stretched triangle of white cloth which had to be the top of a home-made kite.

"A day out," our travelling companion said to the world at large, swallowing the last of a fish-paste sandwich my mother had offered her and twisting her neck to stare up and down the carriage.

Doors slammed, the train shuddered convulsively, and we emerged from the station's cathedral gloom into the dazzle of afternoon sun. "And why not, I'd like to know." She straightened back into her seat. "A treat for the kiddies now this war's at an end." Then, and again speaking to nobody in particular, she added, "Exeter took a pounding."

"'Er certainly did", someone standing nearby agreed.

But my mother, her book packed away with the remnants of our lunch, wasn't listening.

"Not long now," she told us.

She was sitting bolt upright, her voice tense, almost quivering. "Newton Abbot, then Teignmouth, then it's *our* station. Torquay."

Not wanting to meet her strained smile, I was staring out of the window to my right, fixing my attention on fields that looked far greener, lusher, and more undulant than those of Leicestershire. And the full-uddered cattle standing in the shade of trees were unlike the black-and-white Friesians I was used to. These cows were tawny coloured, and, surely, larger, more swag-bellied, their horns wider, more generously curved.

A curtain wall of red clay slid across, blocking my view.

And then, suddenly, people were all turning the other way, someone called out "Dawlish Warren", and my mother was saying, even shouting, her voice thick with emotion—"Look, *look*, both of you, *do* look."

And at last, reluctantly, dreading the churning of gutter water John had predicted, I looked.

— But there was no sea.

Instead, in every direction, the sky had fallen onto the earth, covering it completely, there *was* no earth, there was nothing but this blue that went on forever.

And, yes, I was dazed, astounded, bewildered.

Stunned.

So We Beat on

Of course, it *wasn't* them. For one thing, the couple who'd just disappeared through the wrought-iron gates were assuredly middle-aged. For another, they weren't wearing the right clothes. Barbour jackets didn't exist in 1940, nor would the man have been bare-headed. As for the woman, her head and shoulders protected by the umbrella's translucent cupola — and *that* had to be of recent date — she was both too tall, and moved, not with bustling short steps but a casual grace that was almost a lope.

And the weather was wrong. This was a rainy spring Saturday, whereas that Saturday — it *had* been a Saturday, surely — was sunny, although cloud shadows occasionally darkened the wide lawn that stretched from house to the open gates as I now came up to them, shadows which, I remember thinking, seemed in their passing to drape a veil over the faces of the village crowd gathered for that afternoon's display.

I turned to glance at the church on the other side of the road where, a lifetime earlier, I'd sung in the choir. Should I see if it was open?

Deciding against, I turned back to what was ahead of me and was startled.

The couple had disappeared.

How?

How had they managed to vanish so completely? Could they already be inside the house? No, surely not, there wouldn't have been time for them to cover the distance from gate to front door.

I looked more carefully at the house. That grey, three-storey building standing back from the bevelled, oval lawn was unchanged from the days I had passed it on my way to and from junior school sixty or so years ago. And the lawn, too, was as wide and deep as I remembered, the stone sundial still there at its centre and still splashed by orange-brown lichen, and, yes, still surrounded by curved gravel paths where once the villagers had stood to watch.

And now, shivering at a sudden blast of chill, April wind, I could recall the lengths of hose, like gigantic tapeworms, as they writhed across the lawn. And there, too, in memory, were the firemen in their dark serge-blue with curved helmets like the helmets I imagined cavalrymen once to have worn, scurrying about, aiming their brass nozzles at nothing in particular, or so at first it seemed, and leaving me free to imagine that the polished metal might be strange musical instruments which, as the hose pipes filled and jerked in their grasp, would begin to spray music into the air.

But what came out was water, sputtering, gargling, vomiting, then settling to a steady stream, and as it did so, the firemen directed their hoses to fill galvanised steel buckets which they then distributed among villagers along with dark, metal tubes that my father told me were foot pumps.

I blinked, cleared my gaze. *Was* that large, three-storey house I was looking at through a mist of rain still called the Manor House. There was some sort of armorial shield attached to one of the gates, I saw now; underneath it, worked in black-painted metal, the initials RB.

RB? But hadn't the owners been called Iliffe? Were the couple who had gone through the gates the place's inheritors or were they comparative newcomers who had bought the house and grounds when the former owners died or could no longer afford to live there?

Or might they be casual visitors? Or friends of the present owners?

Whatever, the question of their sudden disappearance remained. *Could* they already be indoors, and if so were they perhaps now studying from a curtained window the figure who stood before the gates, wondering why on earth an aged man should be looking so attentively toward the house, unprotected from rain that was beginning to fall more heavily.

Or had they chosen to hide somewhere behind the tall laurel shrubs that backed those gravelled ways surrounding the lawn?

No, of course not.

Let me view you, then.

But no one left and no one came.

Turning my back on the house, I stared across the road, not now at All Saints but beyond it to where the Manor House farm buildings still loomed above the brick wall running along this part of the village's main street. Behind the farm there had been fields, stretching all the way down to the road where my parents found that small house intended as temporary accommodation — I had a memory of crouching on bare boards in order to peer excitedly between my father's legs at open French windows as he said "Well, it'll do for the while" — but where in the event I, my sister, younger by some eighteen months than me, and mother, were to live for seven years.

Later that day in 1940 we'd walked, all four of us, across those fields, now built over. It was the last day we would be together as a family before my father went away to war. Someone must have told my parents that the Manor House lawn was to be the stage for a display by firemen who would demonstrate to the whole village how to deal with the effect of incendiary bombs or explosives that might at any time be dropped on our houses, and by the time we arrived two hundred or so villagers were already assembled on the gravelled paths, watching firemen explain the drill we'd be expected to follow. I held my father's hand as he said "This is where you'll be safe while I'm gone."

We'd come that day from Coventry. My father had been moved from his work there some months before the bombing of the city, a move my always fearful mother suggested was the only stroke of good luck we could expect. Coventry, where I would later learn from her that streets of houses, included the one we briefly lived in, had been smashed to pieces. And nearby Leicester and not far-off Birmingham, they, too, were names I would hear her utter, always with the same dread inflection.

But the village was spared. In the years that followed our arrival one or two bombs fell in nearby fields, but the closest any of them came to causing us anxiety was when a German plane, eager to lighten its load as it rumbled through the night sky back to the fatherland from a bombing raid somewhere to our west, jettisoned a bomb which landed at the bottom of our road and fractured a water pipe. The bomb failed to explode, and the following day, after it had been made safe, I stood with other boys watching as men dug a trench to get at the pipe, and one boy, Fred Connolly, was reprimanded by an adult when he called out, "Fucking Fritz".

Now, on this rainy April afternoon, I stood facing the Manor House, my gaze shifting from window to window. They stared back, those windows, curtainless, blank. And there was nothing about the white-columned portico to suggest that anyone had recently stood on the shallow step leading up to the porch or opened and then closed its black-painted, grandly sized double doors.

The chill rain and sudden whip of wind again made me shiver.

I shouldn't have come.

Then why had I? Pure chance. No, not true. Or rather, I had made the chance, had turned off from the road I'd been on in order to re-visit a place whose name, glimpsed on a signpost, had, I almost succeeded in persuading myself, tugged of its own accord at the steering wheel until I had no choice but to follow the lane into the village, with the result that as I drove between hedgerows and their no-man's rivers of grass verges I'd not allowed myself to acknowledge that there was any purpose to where this was leading.

Was there a purpose? If so, what?

Ghost hunter? Exorcist? But I hadn't invented the couple I'd seen turning in at the Manor House gates. They were solid flesh. They were innocent of involvement with me, had no connection with those hidden, unexpendable, entirely useless memories of an afternoon lit by spring sun and, for me, a happiness I could not know my parents failed to share.

Time to go.

Two minutes' walk brought me to where I'd left my car, parked across from the church. Opening the driver's door, I paused for one last look up the road.

As if on cue, the couple stepped from between the Manor House gates and, in the steady downpour, strode briskly away from me.

I watched until they turned a corner and were finally out of sight, then I ducked into my car.

Releasing the hand-brake, I heard myself say, "That's the last of it."

But even so I had for some minutes to sit there, behind the driver's wheel, moved by some emotion I couldn't analyse, couldn't understand, feared to let go of, before I could squeeze water from my eyes in order to continue my journey.

Fish and Beans

My first drink of the day. Nikos brought it out to me almost before I'd chosen my seat. The same seat as always, but you have to pretend you've considered other possibilities. Spooning ice cubes into the glass, I watched the liquid begin to turn smokey white, and as it did I caught the sharp, rising scent of aniseed, and only then allowed myself to look out across the harbour to where the lowering sun bled on a sharp edge of the Northern Taygetos. Soon it would disappear behind the mountains, and the sea, for this moment a glaucous, seemingly transparent shimmer, would turn first carnelian, then magenta, then dark blue, and finally, but not before I'd finished my ouzo, become a tarry black.

"No sign of the *Demetrios*," I said, choosing an olive from the saucer of mezes—slices of hard-boiled egg, cheese, sardine—Nikos had found room for on the small, round metal table holding my notebook, glass, bowl of ice-cubes and ashtray. The *Demetrios* was owned by Nikos and his brother, Pedro, though it was the latter who fished. Nikos ran the bar which, like the boat, had been inherited from their father.

"Pedro, he went early," Nikos said. "There are mullet at Tourlo." Like me, he was gazing after the few fishing boats puttering out from harbour.

"I thought Tourlo was off limits?"

Nikos turned to me, smiled briefly, then went back to looking out to sea. "Yes, Tourlo is off limits. Of course." he shrugged.

"But Pedro, he is friends with the naval captain, Mr. Kaprilos. And Mr Kaprilos, he likes mullet. And so…."

Another shrug, a casual, undulant movement of his hand—this is the way things go—and he turned and went back into the dark interior of his waterside bar.

I looked over the water. Manoeuvring among sleek, expensive, sea-going yachts which at this time of year infested the inner harbour, were the little one or at most two-man crewed boats, *Maria*, *Athena*, *Nikolaos*, others I didn't recognise, all puttering off to their nightwork, some no doubt heading for the far side of the island, in search of mullet, others steering for waters further down the Saronic Gulf. Everyone agreed that this part of the Mediterranean was rapidly emptying of its once plentiful stocks: galeos, atherina, gavros, mourouna, and, yes, mullet, both grey and, above all, the red, its succulent white flesh a rare delight, its name proudly displayed on the chalked board of any taverna lucky enough to have a newly caught supply.

The fish were disappearing, but still, every evening, the fishermen set out. And the next morning, as they sat over their coffee, they would spread their hands in that supplicatory manner more eloquent than any words as they compared their experiences of a night's fishing that had brought little reward for most of them. "We need a miracle. Agios Nektarios must help us."

And really, what chance did the island's small boats stand against the factory ships that sailed out from Italian and Spanish ports? A few days earlier, having accepted an offer to join a cluster of old sea captains I knew as they sat hunched at a waterfront kafeneion, I'd listened to a cautionary tale of two fishermen undone by greed. They had, I was told, taken out their boat one night and, having netted a reasonable catch, decided to try for more. Let us make our fortune. But why, they'd asked each other, go to the bother of fishing with nets? Why not instead lob overboard a stick of dynamite, blow the fish out of the water and gather them up when they surfaced, stunned, many of them dead from shock. Good idea.

No, bad idea, very bad. The dynamite must have gone off too soon, because when, the following morning, after they'd failed to return, a boat went out to search for them, all that was found were the charred remains of body parts floating in the water near the fishermen's empty vessel. "So you see," the man who narrated the story ended sententiously, "we should take from the sea only what is needed for our lives."

There were nods of approval from all those grouped at the table, murmurs of "bravo."

The fact that for many years men had regularly used dynamite to blow fish out of the water was not mentioned, and it would have been uncivil to ask how anyone could have known what the soon-to-be dynamited fishermen had said to each other. Nor did I reveal that earlier in the summer, when I had been on Leros, I had heard from fishermen there an identical tale, nor was I prepared to mention that a friend on a brief visit to Paros brought back a similar story, this one relating to the fishermen of Anti-Paros. Perhaps, who knows, there was a tale that could be traced to an actual source, though by now, after constant re-telling, it had turned into myth. The gods punish those who over-reach themselves. Midas, Niobe, Prometheus, Icarus, Tantalus, avaricious fishermen. Christian morality braided with classical lore. When someone is near death, an islander will tell you, shrugging fatalistically as he does so, that the dying man or woman is battling Charon.

***

Was it brooding on such matters that made me aware of the old couple, the only other occupants of Nikos's at that early evening hour? They sat some tables away, further back, unmistakeably of the island. He was in black jacket, tie-less white shirt buttoned at the neck, she wore widow's black, her grey hair in a severe bun. Risking a look—but they were absorbed in their conversation—I wondered whether, deep in shadow though they were, I might recognise either of them? Not her, certainly. She was in three-quarters profile, listening and occasionally nodding at his words, her large eyes staring down at the coffee cup which she made no attempt to lift to her lips, not even at those moments when, hands raised from her lap as if in silent agreement, she would glance up at something he had said, permitting herself a brief smile that was gone as suddenly as it lightened that otherwise grave, immobile face.

As for him, it was possible I'd seen him among those men who took their coffee each morning at one of the several waterfront bars, but then again, the grey cap under which thick grey hair frizzed out, his long, tanned and wrinkled face, was of a type so familiar as to be virtually indistinguishable from that of other retired "sea-captains", as they were mostly called, even though some, perhaps most, had never been in a boat except for those occasions when they paid a visit to the mainland.

What was he saying, the old man? Something to do with the sea, a boat, fish. *Thalassa, psarovarka, psari.* Perhaps he had overheard Nikos's explanation for the early departure of the *Demetrios*, and was reporting to his companion something of the perils that came from fishing in a spot the Greek navy reserved for its own purposes. Danger, he was saying. *Kindeenos.*

But no, he was using the past tense. "It was dangerous. Those were dangerous times." And now, hands again raised, she was nodding her agreement. All Greek gestures mean something, all are eloquent, but that particular gesture, hands raised in parallel to chest level, palms open, fingers outstretched and tilted slightly upwards as though to receive a skein of wool, is especially lovely. A gesture of full-hearted acquiescence, implying, as circumstances require, grieved or comic acceptance of fate.

What was that? *Hoffman*? Commandant Hoffman? Ah, yes, now I knew. They were talking about the German army's occupation of the island in 1941. That was when the fortress of Tourlo had been constructed to act as look-out post and gun emplacement for the Germans. From there the occupiers had an uninterrupted view of sea and sky, could observe planes or boats approaching from the mainland or, for that matter, from the western Aegean. And the bay below Tourlo was where Pedro, Nikos's brother and joint owner, with him, of the *Demetrius*, was now heading, while Nikos, as always, tended the bar the brothers would, in time, pass to their sons.

I strained to listen, but now four young tourists arrived, two men, two women, and sat at a table between me and the old couple.

Nikos waited patiently to take their orders while they arranged their chairs to face out over the harbour. A nailparing of moon stood above the islet a mile across the water from where we sat, and, in the small port further along the waterfront, a ferry, deck lights triangulating the violet sky, was beginning to open its bow door, "like a whale getting ready to swallow plankton", one of the newcomers observed.

"Or spew out a bellyful of cars."

"Alan, dear, you're such a romantic." A woman's voice, that. They all laughed.

Nikos brought their drinks, then, tray tucked under an arm, came to join me, his back to them and to the old couple beyond.

"Who are they, do you know?" I asked as he lit a cigarette. "Not the ones at the next table, the old couple."

Nikos looked briefly to where I gestured, then back at me. "Mr Antonio and Mrs Sophia. Old friends. They have not met for sixty years."

"Eh?" Had I misunderstood? "Old friends who've not met for over half a century. *Never?*"

Perhaps misunderstanding my question, Nikos said, "They met by chance in the street yesterday. It is OK. She is a widow, he is a widower."

"No, I mean, if they were friends how come they've not seen anything of each other in all that time. Has one of them—have both of them—been living abroad?" Islanders did often take ship in order to find work in foreign parts, many of them, though by no means all, intending to return in old age to their place of birth. Keeping Ithaka always in their mind.

But Nikos said, "No, no, they stay here, they don't go nowhere. But Mr Antonio, he is from a wealthy family and Mrs Sophia, she is not. They loved each other. But it was impossible. So they marry different people. And her husband, he like to keep Mrs Sophia indoors when he is alive. You know."

"Men must work and women must sweep."

Ignoring my attempt at wit, Nikos said, "They are pleased to see each other."

"They've much to talk about," I said. "They seem to be speaking about the war. The German occupation. Is that it?"

Nikos nodded. "Mr Antonio, when he was young he work to help build the fortress at Tourlo. And Sophia, she was a hospital nurse."

"Here?"

"Yes. The Germans took over a hotel, made it a hospital for themselves. Not for islanders. Though, you know, some medicines can go out. They disappear. But it is dangerous. As dangerous as taking things from the fortress. If you are discovered you go to Piraeus. There the Gestapo are. Then, pouff." He aimed two fingers at my heart.

"Mr Antonio, he made mention of a Commandant Hoffman. Hoffman was the German officer in charge, wasn't he?"

"People say he was not a bad man," Nikos said. "Who knows? He saved some islanders from death, but others…"

He shrugged, then crushed his cigarette into the now empty saucer, careful to brush away the few crumbs of ash that had fallen onto my open notebook, and both of us turned to look beyond the occupants of the next table at the old couple, who were now laughing at some shared memory, Sophia wiping her eyes with the heel of her hand as she shook her head in a kind of comic disbelief at the story she and her companion were sharing.

Nikos nodded and smiled. "They talk now of Polyfava", he said. "Many Beans." Then he, too, laughed.

"Many Beans," he said again. He tapped his forehead. "A good boy, but, you know."

I could guess. The island had more than its share of mental or physical retards, especially among the older population, products of a genetic flaw, some said, though others spoke darkly of the dangers of inter-marriage.

"Does he come into town?"

Nikos shook his head. "Many Beans, he is dead. He is dead a long time ago."

"And why his nickname?" In the not so distant past, islanders habitually gave nicknames to each other, but these were customarily linked to occupation—"Pistachio Man", "Meat Cleaver", or dress—"Wooden Clogs", "Short Pants", "Leather Cap", or physical appearance—"Seven Bellies", "Black September". This last was a recently dead wastrel whose swarthy complexion, linked to the month of his birth, marked him out for fearful opprobrium. People finding themselves near Black September were quick to make contact with the blue bead they carried with them at all times. The bead might be set in a necklace or bracelet or carried in a pocket. But it had to be within reach. A blue bead to ward off the evil eye.

But Many Beans? Full of beans? Did it perhaps mean, as in English usage, someone bursting with good health? No, no, Nikos explained, laughing, the name came about because from his early years Polyfava always carried in his pocket dried carob pods, "and, you know, he ate them to keep alive."

Carob trees grew all over the island. I had heard that the tree's fruit was what saved the islanders from starving in large numbers during the terrible winter of 1941. I said as much to Nikos.

He nodded. "But the miracle of the fish helped more."

"The fish?"

"That was what Mr Antonio was talking about with Mrs Sophia. You didn't hear?"

"I heard something about the sea being full of fish. I thought he might be talking about the *Demetrios*. You know, fishing off limits."

"No." Nikos lit another cigarette. Nikos the story-teller, Nikos *Afygitis*, was settling in for talk. "No, the fish. A miracle of Saint Nektarios." Nektarios, the island's saint, dead in the earlier years of the twentieth century, to whom several miraculous acts were attributed. In his revered memory what seemed to me a spectacularly ugly church had been built in the mountainous centre of the island, where it became a regular place of pilgrimage for coachloads of tourists and mainlanders. The saint's hospital robe, given to a dying man, was said to have returned the sufferer to the full vigour of his life. But the miracle of the fish? What was that?

A big miracle, Nikos said, the biggest of them all.

The four at the next table were preparing to leave. Nikos swivelled to watch as, getting to their feet, they scattered coins on the table, raised a hand in salutation when he wished them good evening, but made no other move. He was intent on telling me about the fish. This is what he said.

It was the winter of 1941. In living memory there had never been a time of such terrible cold. The end of the world, some prophesied. A series of storms covered the island in icy snow, right down to the water's edge. The crops were killed off. The animals—goats, sheep, horses, donkeys, poultry—all died. The people began to die. They died at home, they dropped dead in the streets. Two doctors, working for nothing, went from village to village, doing what they could. But they had little by way of medicine, the Germans would give them nothing, and the food stores were soon exhausted. A few villagers in the middle of the island had hoarded supplies of olive oil, but not enough to sustain even a small family for long, and certainly not sufficient to last through those months of unending cold. There was death everywhere and the corpses lay in their shrouds, unburied.

The German soldiers were fed, of course, their supplies came into the frozen harbour from Piraeus. But for the islanders, nothing, nothing.

Then, one morning, someone came running into one of the kaefenions where men sat huddled. Quick, they were told, come quick. The harbour is full of fish.

Fish, what fish? Disbelieving, the men all rushed down to the waterfront to see for themselves.

And it was true, fish everywhere. Nikos spoke as though he himself had seen the miracle. The thumb and index finger he held aloft almost touched. Tiny fish, no bigger than shrimps. They covered the surface of the sea, threshing about, millions of them, yes, millions. Pails were fetched, dipped into icy sea-water that was crammed so tight with the fish it seemed a heaving blanket of silver covered the entire harbour. Experienced fishermen inspected the filled pails, poked their fingers among the tiny bodies, lifted some out and rested them on the palms of their hands, sniffed them. Nikos opened his own palm, stared at invisible fish. Nobody had ever seen these before, nobody had a name for them. They weren't shellfish, they had fins and tails, and mouths that opened and shut as they gasped for air. And of course, Nikos said, the men wanted to know if the fish were safe to eat.

There was only one way to find out. One of the captains took a pail of fish up to his house, got his wife to boil the contents and then—Nikos smiled faintly—ordered her to taste what she had cooked. When he saw there were no ill effects, the captain too ate. Then he ran down to the harbour front to tell the people now gathered there that the fish could be eaten. Soon, people from all over the island were hurrying to the waterfront with pails, tin cans, saucepans, whatever they could find. And, wonder of wonders, no matter how many people scooped up the fish, the supply never failed. If anything, it seemed to increase, even spread beyond the harbour walls to the outer sea. The fish were too tiny to grill, so people made them into soups or fried them to make patties or simply pounded them into a kind of paste. They were not very good-tasting, but they saved lives.

"People's bellies were filled, children were spared from crying out in hunger, nursing mothers could once again make milk."

"And the German army? They allowed this?"

"Why you ask that?"

"Because," I said, "I heard that islanders were shot if they took fish from the sea. The fish were reserved for the occupiers."

"It is true," Nikos said. "But Commandant Hoffman, he let the people take these fish. He don't stop them. He don't let the soldiers shoot."

"So thanks to him they survived? Hoffman the good Nazi."

Nikos nodded. "And then," he said, "one day, the spring comes." Up went the hands. "The snow melts, the sun it warms the island. And the fish—the fish disappears."

The hands spread in a grand flourish. "A miracle." Word and gesture were consummate, spontaneous, and long practised.

"You mean, the fish never returned? What, *never*?"

"*Never.*"

Nikos was staring gravely at me, unblinking. "A miracle," he repeated. "*Malempi*, we called the fish."

"Which means miracle?"

"No, no," Nikos said, "Miracle is *thavma*. But it *was* a miracle."

I was silent. But then a question occurred. What had Polyfava to do with this? Had he been the first to see the fish, perhaps? Or hear rumours?

"Polyfava? No, no." Nikos laughed.

The sound of chairs being scraped across gravel made us both turn to look at the table where, I now saw, the four I thought had already left were standing as though at attention, staring at us, or rather at Nikos. They had been listening to his tale and, as he glanced enquiringly toward them, the two women began to clap, hesitantly, smiling, as though the story had been laid on for their benefit. Perhaps it had.

Nikos, bowing slightly, tray in hand, went to scoop up their money, then, as they said their farewells and slowly, reluctantly, I thought, moved away, he gathered together their empty glasses and wiped the table clean with a quick flick of his hand.

When he came to rejoin me, a single glass on his tray, he was laughing. The solemnity that had been appropriate to his telling of the miracle of the fish had disappeared. Now he had a different tale to tell.

Handing me the glass, he said, "With compliments. Please to drink while I tell you about Polyfava. This is, shall we say, another story. One that belongs to the years after the German army has gone."

He rested the edge of the tray on the table where I sat, watched me sip the contents—raki—and glanced over to where the old couple were still laughing at their reminiscences, calling across to them, "I will tell our friend about Polyfava?"

"Yes, yes," they said between laughs, "tell him." And Mr Antonio, raising his right hand, twisted it slightly, a gesture of goodwill. I give you my permission, the gesture said.

"Well," Nikos said, turning back to me. "So I will tell you what happens and why we laugh." He paused, as though considering how to begin, or perhaps he was waiting for my nod of assent. I leant back in my chair, spread my hands. "Please," I said. "I want to hear."

But Nikos was already speaking. "Polyfava, as I say, is a good boy, but when he is thirty he still is inexperienced in women. You understand?" Another pause while he glanced at me. "OK. So some friends want to change this, make him a man." He paused yet again, pretending to consider his words. "So what they do, they save up for his birthday and take him on the ferry to Piraeus so he can visit a brothel. You pay for your ferry ticket, they tell him, and the rest is free. They know some of the girls at this brothel, nice girls, and it is all arranged. Then, it comes to Polyfava's birthday and off they go, Polyfava in a straw hat to look good."

Nikos drew a pack of cigarettes from his apron pocket, selected one, and, only after he had lit it and inhaled deeply, went on. "Well, Polyfava, he has a good time. He has a *very* good time. He has such a good time he decides that he will save up to buy a ferry ticket for another trip to the brothel. So he does, and a month later he is on the ferry to Piraeus once again with his straw hat. Naturally, people on the boat, who know him, they ask him where he is going and why is he looking so happy. So he tells them. 'Ah, I had such a nice time at the brothel last month I am going there again.'

"'Well, good for you, Polyfava,' they say. 'But what will you do for money? Can you afford a visit to the brothel?'

"'No need,' Polyfava tells them, 'it is free.'

"Now of course the story of his birthday treat has gone around the island so the people he's talking to think they had better explain to him. 'Friends paid for you last time,' they say, 'but this time you will have to pay for yourself.'"

Another pause, this time while Nikos shaded his eyes to look over the water to where the dark shape of a tour boat, strung with lights like a floating hotel, appeared round the headland and curved silently in to port. But soon enough he lost interest in it, shrugged, and came back to his tale.

"Polyfava, he is confused, his mind is tangled. He has been greatly looking forward to this day but now it seems it cannot happen. He asks them. 'Are you sure I have to pay? I didn't last time. I thought the brothel was free.'

"'No, no,' he is told. 'You must understand. Your friends paid for you. It was a birthday present. But now you are on your own. You cannot visit a brothel without money.'

"Polyfava is very sad. What can he do? Then comes an idea. He takes off his hat and, holding it out like an old beggar, he goes round the boat explaining to people that he needs money to pay for a visit to the brothel. And you know"—Nikos shook his head in mock wonder—"by the time the boat arrives at Piraeus, Polyfava has enough money—from the women as well as from the men—to pay for at least two more visits to the brothel."

Still laughing, he picked up his tray and made for the bar.

Left alone, I looked across to where the old couple, now on their feet, were shaking hands as they said their farewells to each other. Beyond their black, erect figures, waterfront lights of bars and tavernas spilled into the deepening sky. I raised my hand but I don't think either noticed. They turned from each other, he toward the town, she away from it.

Time I, too, was on my way. Tipping back my glass, I swallowed the last drops of ouzo, then, pocketing my notebook, stood, looking a moment longer over the glimmering patch of harbour water in front of me.

Malempi, Polyfava.

Ah, Greece, Greece.

The Hotel of Dreams

Late March on the island is a special time. Light off the sea is opalescent, the blue-grey mountains on the mainland beyond are still draped with snow that clings, crisp as newly-starched sheets, to the upper slopes, and all across the island pistachio orchards pulse with those nubbles of "fire coal" buds that flare on the trees' angular, gawky. ash-grey branches, as though warming them to renewed life. In addition, fields which later in the year will be mother-earth naked or host clumps of brittle, tawny-gold grasses and sage-green prickly pear, are now patched with yellow daisies, blue ice flowers, and, above all—a truly primal touch—the blood-red poppies that seem at a signal to be jetting out of the soil. Hesperian fables true, if true, here only.

Twenty minutes after stepping ashore from the morning's first ferry and walking the inland road from port town to the village of Faros, I was at my flat, easing open its shutters. Hello, Faros, I'm back.

An hour to sleep off the effects of the overnight flight, a shower, and then, shaved and dressed, I was ready to face the day.

I strolled down the lane, paused at the bottom where it joined the narrow coast road and glanced at the small harbour across the way—most of the fishing boats were ones I recognised, as were the three or four men crouching side by side on rocks, although they were too absorbed in talk to notice my hand raised in salutation—and then paused again to inspect the large, open four-wheel drive parked outside the hotel, its back seat crammed with boxes and cartons. That was new. And though the hotel sign was still not restored, at least the front door was open. Andreas, it appeared, was not only still in business, he must be in funds. Good!

In the dim light of the entrance lobby a stockily-built man, back to me, leant across the high wooden counter, studying rows of pigeon-holes.

"Andreas," I called. "It's me. Peter."

But when the man turned, I saw it wasn't Andreas at all. This man had close-cropped hair, a hatchet-lean face, and as he came across to me I noticed the steel-rimmed spectacles that slightly magnified his eyes. Under the black leather jacket, white T-shirt and faded denims there wasn't a trace of Andreas's comfortable flab. Powerfully muscled, his tanned flesh looked to be honed by regular work-outs. And there was no warmth in his stare.

"Andreas?" he said. "What do you want with Andreas?"

Something in the flat, estuarial voice, the way he pronounced Andreas's name, warned me that I was off limits.

"I dropped by to say hello."

No answer, but the stare was unnerving.

"I've not seen him since last autumn," I said.

"That so." He took his time over looking me up and down. After what seemed several moments he said, and his voice gave nothing away, "Well, he's not here." Then, more emphatically, he added "Andreas isn't around. At the moment. Not now."

"You mean he's not on the island?"

Before he could answer, another man backed into view through the swing door that led, I knew, to the hotel bar beyond the lobby. In his arms he was cradling a large cardboard box from within which came the sound of bottles clinking and jostling against one another.

"Where'd you want these to go, boss?"

Then, turning, he saw me. "Oh, sorry, didn't realise we'd got company."

Without taking his eyes off me, the first man said, "Someone's asking after Andreas."

The second man came close. Shorter than the man he called boss, his black leather jacket hung loose on his scrawny body. He grinned cheerfully through what, even in the lobby's dim light, I could see were tobacco-stained teeth. "Ain't gonna find Andreas 'ere, mate."

"No." The first man spoke slowly and as though for the benefit of all. "That's what I told him. More or less. We don't know where Andreas is, do we?" There was a pause, during which the two men looked unblinkingly at each other. "We don't know, do we. Trevor?"

The short man began to nod, then changed the movement to a shake of his head. "Not a clue."

Now I knew at least one of their names, I decided to repeat my own. "I'm Peter" I said, holding out my hand. "I live up the lane. Well, I live half the year here. The other half I'm in England."

"Bit like us then," the small man said. "Birds of passage, ain't we boss?"

The big man took my hand in his own and his grip, slight though it was, left me in no doubt as to his strength. "John," he said.

"But we call him Big John," the small man said. He was still hugging the box to his chest.

"Welcome to the island," I said.

"Not much of an island," Trevor said, still cheerful. "Can't say I'd fancy spending time here. I took a gander last night. The bar life's a miss, couldn't find a restaurant with a touch of real class, and not many big houses, are there? I never saw a swimming pool, not one."

"That'll do, Trevor," his boss said, unsmiling. "Peter won't be interested in your views of his island." Then, having let my hand go, he turned to the short man. "All for Juliet", he said, nodding at the bottle-crammed cardboard box. "And while you're there, don't forget to give the family a bell. Check everything is OK."

"Whatever you say, boss."

Legs slightly bowed under the weight of his load, Trevor disappeared through the hotel's entrance.

I made to follow him. I wanted to know what had happened to Andreas, why he, who was after all the hotel owner, wasn't here, and why these two *were*, but it seemed plain enough that I wasn't going to get anything out of Big John. Not only that. There was no mistaking the hint in the way he spoke, nor in how he looked at me. He wanted me off the premises.

But then he surprised me. "Fancy a beer?"

It wasn't an especially friendly enquiry, but after a moment's hesitation I accepted. Perhaps after all I was going to be given an explanation for the mystery, as I already thought of it, of Andreas's absence. Besides, I was thirsty. And, also besides, I could hear, distant but unmistakeable, the sound of fishermen's laughter from down at the small harbour, could see beyond the lobby's glass frontage the Saronic sky that stretched, milkily-blue, as far as the mainland's mountain range some three miles across the water, could imagine the day's hesitant, promissory warmth, and despite the prickle of alarm that these men—well, that Big John—caused, the sense that their being here wasn't good for Andreas, I could feel the surge of delight, exultance even, that the island always awoke in me.

So, "Yes," I said, "a beer would be fine."

Turning his head slightly, but without taking his eyes off me, the man called over his shoulder. "Waverley, beers wanted for me and a guest." A pause. "And bring one for yourself and Trev."

Big John led the way to the far side of the lobby, and as I dropped into a chair, one of those small blue-painted chairs that belong as naturally to Greek bars as the aniseed scent of ouzo, a tall, thin figure pushed through the rear swing doors. Balancing four bottles of *Amstel* on a tray, he advanced to where we sat and I saw that under the inevitable black leather jacket he, too, wore a white T-shirt. With what seemed anxious deliberation, he placed the tray on the glass-topped table, one of a dozen I remembered from last summer when Andreas had called me in to approve—"Class, my friend, pure class, for ladies and their cocktails"—while John, sitting opposite, rested his powerful arms on the table so that the sleeves of his jacket rode up slightly and revealed a thin gold bracelet on his left wrist—on the right was one of those watches designed for space travel—and with a curt nod of the head invited the newcomer, who had remained standing, to draw up another chair.

Diffidently, the young man obliged.

"Waverley comes from Canada," John said, as though by way of an explanation.

"Oh? Whereabouts in Canada?" I'd once been invited to a literary festival in Toronto and from there had gone on to Montreal and Vancouver.

"Edmonton," Waverley said at last, looking at John as though seeking permission to speak. Perhaps because his voice was scarcely more than a whisper I could hear no trace in it of a Canadian accent.

John raised his bottle and indicated we should do likewise. We clinked bottles and drank.

"We should do this more often," I said.

Big John dismissed the attempt at humour. "Not much chance of that. A few more hours and we'll be off and out of here."

"So, a fleeting visit", I said, "or have you been here for some time?"

Smiling thinly at my attempt to discover what the presence of the three of them meant, Big John said, as though humouring me, "Let's just say we've called in to attend to Andreas's business for him." A pause while he drank. "Seeing as how he's unable to attend to it himself," he said, wiping his mouth with the back of his hand and getting rid of moisture and smile with the one gesture.

He seemed to be about to leave it at that. But changing his mind, he said, "And as Andreas seems to have owed a lot of people a heap of dosh we're doing our best to repay his debts. All heart, we are." Another pause. "Did he borrow off you?" he asked, as though taking for granted that Andreas owed me money.

As it happened, Andreas did. One morning the previous August I was off to Leros for a few days to see a poet friend, and as I went down the lane, bag slung over my shoulder, Andreas called out to me from the hotel patio. "Mr. Peter? You are going into town, perhaps? Good. Can you help, please? I must to pay the laundry bill. Me, I am tied up here all day and they are shouting for their piddling amount of cash."

"No problem," I told him. "I'll be passing the laundry. You can pay me back at the end of the week."

The bill turned out not to be all that piddling but never mind, Andreas would repay me. As it happened, though, he wasn't at the hotel when I got back from Leros, where I'd spent far longer than the short visit I'd intended. Nor had he reappeared when, at the end of September, I left the island and flew back to England. But I wasn't going to bring this up now, not with Big John.

"If anything," I said, "it's the other way round. I owe Andreas."

"You *do?*"

"Certainly I do." And I told him why.

Two summers before I had fallen into conversation with a Greek on the ferry to Piraeus. In reply to his casual question, more polite than genuinely enquiring, or so I thought, I explained that I spent every summer on the island. "A good place to write," I said, adding that the one drawback was that so far I'd failed to locate a decent flat to rent and had therefore to make use of hotels. "And in summer even a modest-sized hotel room can be pricey." At which point the man, who now introduced himself as Andreas Karoulis, told me that behind a hotel he owned, Hotel Zeus, the only hotel in a village not far from the port town, there was a small complex of self-sufficient flats for rent "at very good prices," and that the administrator for the complex could be contacted at a telephone number he now wrote down—a London one—adding that as far as he knew some apartments were still available.

"So as soon as I was back in England," I told Big John, "I phoned the number and that's how I now come to be here."

Which was true, although I didn't add that I'd had some trouble deciphering the ill-shaped numbers Andreas had set down on the paper I produced. Nor did I mention that he had ham-fistedly all but wrecked the nib of my fountain pen.

Only one part of my story interested the man opposite. "He said he 'owned' this hotel?" The question had a sardonic edge to it.

"I think so."

Big John gave a faint smile, more a slight twist of his thin lips. "Some of us *don't* think so," he said....

Then he stopped.

I turned to follow his gaze. Trevor was beckoning to his boss from the lobby entrance.

John levered himself up from his seat and went across to where Trevor waited, while Waverley and I sat, our gazes shifting from mutual inspection to the two men who stood, heads together in whispered conversation.

After some minutes John gave Trevor what was, I suppose, meant as a reassuring pat between the shoulder blades, though it also functioned as a push to send him on his way. "'Fraid we'll have to break off the pleasantries" he said, as he rejoined us. "I've a bit of urgent business to attend to. Trev tells me the kids back home aren't minding my business like they should." He waited for me to say something, and when I didn't added, "Families, eh? Don't you just love 'em."

It didn't sound as though he loved his.

"Waverley, on your feet. We need you."

I got to mine.

"Here." John reached and gave me the nearly-full bottle of beer. "Take this with you. No point in wasting good drink."

There was clearly no time to waste on goodbyes, either. He was anxious to have me off the premises.

Taking the bottle, I said, "Well, in case I don't see you again...."

"Like I said, we've about finished here."

"So you'll be off home?"

"Who knows," John said. "Barcelona or Billericay. A difficult call." And for the first and only time he laughed. A mirthless laugh, but still, a laugh for all that.

***

Later that morning, after I had walked into town the back way and shopped for a few basic provisions, I sat in one of my favourite waterfront bars sipping an ouzo, my attention caught by a large motor yacht anchored out in the bay. Most boats of that size came in during the high summer season, filling the outer harbour with canned music and the sounds of rich laughter. What had Nick Carraway said of Daisy Buchanan? Her voice was full of money. He should have heard the lot who came here. Minor film stars, Russian billionaires, Middle-Eastern oil-rich sheiks, living it up while we people on the promenade looked at them. I watched the ocean-going yacht as it lifted on a slight swell, its prow pointing to shore, radar scanner turning implacably, antennae glittering like black threads in the blue Aegean sky.

A slight breeze shifted the boat so that it began to swing round until I could see the painted name on its side.

JULIET.

Click.

So that was where the stuff stripped out of the Hotel Zeus was going. And then? The answer was obvious. Big John and his henchmen would be heading back to where, in contrast to this island, there were big houses, bars with classy music, swimming pools. Costa del Crime. Barcelona or Billericay? Not a difficult call, not at all. But whatever had brought them here couldn't be good for Andreas. Was this what was meant by asset stripping? What had Andreas done, or not done, to warrant the removal of valuables from his hotel. And where *was* Andreas? "He's not around." What had Big John meant by those words? And why had he shown such disdain—contempt almost—when I'd spoken of Andreas as the hotel's owner.

"I own the Hotel Zeus" Or. "The Hotel Zeus is mine, please to know." Andreas's gutteral, croaky voice would be filled with pride when he spoke the words, as he always did when identifying himself. Or, if he was seeking to impress guests with his status, "The hotel you have come to, of which I happen to be owner."

Owner was what he'd called himself when we first met on the ferry. But then I remembered that the business card he gave me as we prepared to dock at Piraeus—digging it out from a black leather wallet stuffed with papers—identified him as "Executive Director of the *Hotel Zeus*". At the time, I hadn't thought about the different nomenclature. Owner. Executive Director. Same difference. But later, as rumours of his money difficulties began to spread across the island, they were accompanied by suggestions that Andreas was at best managing the hotel for a Greek family who owned both hotel and apartments and who lived in London.

Ah, yes, Andreas and money. Andreas and his dreams.

When, after our chance meeting on the ferry, he and I had stepped ashore at Piraeus, I held out my hand, intending to thank him for telling me about the apartments, and to say goodbye to him and his wife, who stood silently by his side.

But Andreas had other ideas. "Come," he said, hooking his hand under my outstretched arm, "I have something to show you. Something *important*." And he steered me across the blisteringly hot quayside to a small bar I knew from early morning stopovers to or from the airport as a haunt for night owls and waterfront characters looking for the chance to bum a drink.

Once the three of us were settled at a table near the back of the bar, Andreas cleared a space in order to lay flat on the table's surface the large, heavy-duty, plastic-encased portfolio he had held onto throughout our brief sea journey. A quick glance round as though to satisfy himself we weren't being spied on, then he laid before me some architectural drawings. I had barely taken these in before he whisked them away and in their place spread out coloured topographical sketches of two islands, showing a number of buildings, ranging from small cottage-style houses to three-storey constructions, civic in appearance.

In answer to my unasked question, Andreas named the islands.

What, *those?* The drawings implied that the islands were large, mountainous, extensive. In fact they were not much more than grass-thatched rocks extruding into the bay waters of the island's port town. The Aegean is thronged with such islets, literally thousands of them, surviving fragments of vast earth movements, bits of land broken off from the larger masses that form the nation's habitable islands. Fishermen use some to shelter from the sudden storms that can explode in the Aegean at any time of year, but for the most part they are home only to birds and the occasional colony of seals or, more rarely, turtles.

Perhaps Andreas sensed my disbelief, because, from peering short-sightedly at the drawings, he now straightened up and stared at me, his face tense with an emotion I couldn't identify. A stubby forefinger stabbed at the drawing which featured a white-tiled building with spacious windows and, in front of it, a stretch of sloping lawn. "That," he said, "will be a hospital. And this," lifting up another drawing for my inspection, "do you know what this is?"

"It looks like a golf course."

"Exactly. A golf course. Please to notice the chalets surrounding it." He paused. "And I am going to build both hospital and golf course. One for one island, one for the other."

"Really? But how? I mean they're surely too small." By several miles, I might have added. Was this some sort of joke?

But Andreas waved away my incredulity.

"My architect has permission to dynamite and level the islands. That will give us all the space we need. Then our building can commence. Anything is possible."

And now, his wife, whom Andreas introduced as Jane, a plump English woman with a sweet, puppyish face, spoke, her public school accent surprising me as much as her actual words. "Andreas can do *anything*," she said, her voice ardent with what seemed genuine belief in the man who sat smiling across at me. If you don't believe me, his smile said, you will surely believe her.

"Andreas will forbid motor transport on either island," Jane told me. It sounded as though she was reading from a brochure. "All movement is to be by horse and cart. Like Hydra and Spetses. Andreas will return island Greece to how it used to be. The government has agreed that he can start the work whenever he wants. The EU is in favour. They welcome schemes that increase provision of public health."

Why ever did I believe them? Partly, I suppose, because Jane so clearly believed him, believed *in* him. How else explain why a woman who would have seemed quite at home on the cover of *Country Life*, flower-filled trug on arm and mullion-windowed house glimpsed past bevelled lawn and clipped yew, should now be gazing devotedly at this squat, fleshy man in an ill-fitting black suit, dark, frog-like eyes behind horn-rimmed spectacles somehow enhanced by the croaky words with which he explained that the Hotel Zeus was to be part of the transformation he planned.

At the time, the hotel was a derelict-looking hulk, one I would pass on walks out of town when I'd take the coast road to the village of Faros with its tiny harbour. It seemed permanently shut, forlorn, like so many Greek buildings that had been put up in speculative hope and then abandoned when whoever built them ran out of funds or discovered a new dream, a more assured way of making a fortune.

"The Hotel Zeus is in a terrible state of disrepair," I said, hoping he would not be offended. But Andreas nodded complacently. Soon, he said, as he put back and zipped up the drawings, it would be the island's most desirable hotel. And in future years guests would be taken by caique to the golf course where overnight accommodation could be arranged. Hence, the cottages—chalets, Andreas called them—and although the architect hadn't as yet devised an exclusive taverna, this would be ready for when the golf course opened.

And the hospital?

At once, Andreas's voice became urgent with sincerity. "My poor mother, she died in a bad hospital in Athens. Very bad. No care was taken for her. She was in pain. I cannot tell you." His fist slammed down on the table. "I make this hospital in her memory. Poor people must have their dignity." The anger was genuine, so, too, the tears that glimmered behind his thick spectacles.

Was that the clincher? Common sense told me that Andreas's plans were mere fantasy. Nobody could build a golf course on a piece of rocky land which was at most a hundred yards square, let alone surround it with chalets. There wasn't even enough space for a pitch and putt course. And how could you have a hospital of any size on a sterile slab of granite even smaller in size than the other islet? As to horse-drawn carriages....

I looked at the portfolio of drawings Andreas had propped by his chair, then I looked at him, and then I looked away. I didn't want to meet the challenge in those eyes, the way he was daring me to disbelieve him.

It was all madness. It *had* to be madness.

And yet there was an air of such conviction in the way he spoke that common sense seemed beside the point. He plainly believed what he was saying, and who was I to doubt him. Besides, I think, no I'm certain, that I wanted to believe him. More even than that, I wanted him to succeed.

***

And for a while at least it seemed that at least part of his dream was coming true.

When I arrived on the island the following June—publication of a new book had delayed my usual spring arrival—I took a taxi to the village. It was early afternoon, too hot to walk, and I was beginning to nod off when the driver brought his taxi to a dramatic halt at the bottom of my lane.

"Big changes, eh?" he said, pointing out of his open window. "Mr Andreas, he is a man who makes things happen."

"I think so," I said as I followed his gaze. And then, vision clearing, I said it again.

The hotel had been—well, I won't say transformed, because, given its obdurate, ungainly length, its look of a beached, abandoned liner, that would have been impossible—but Andreas had certainly made things happen.

Early afternoon sun gave the hotel an almost surreal, pristine look. The plaster in which the brickwork was encased, and which I remembered as grey and splotched from years of neglect, was now a smoothly rendered white; lengths of previously exposed, rusted piping were hidden behind white cladding; the formerly shabby woodwork now gleamed sky-blue; there were fresh white curtains at each window; and an entirely new awning over the entrance, buttercup yellow, had, stretched above it, a banner proclaiming HOTEL ZEUS WELCOMES YOU.

Nor was that all. Clambering from the taxi, I saw that the hotel's taverna, once a desolate slab of concrete perched above the harbour and directly across the road from the front patio, was now shaded by a canopy under which a group of locals was sipping ouzo, and at other tables what had to be hotel guests who had come up from the sea, plainly intent on a long, leisurely meal, were being shown to tables by waiters in the conventional garb of white shirt and black trousers. Other guests, most of them in swimsuits, sprawled on the hotel's upper balconies, smoking and gazing down at those below or shaded their eyes to follow the paths of yachts that filleted the Saronic Gulf or swung toward shore in slow white curves.

I was about to gather up my bags when a voice from the hotel stopped me.

"Mister Peter, Mister Peter."

Wearing his familiar baggy black suit, Andreas was waving to me from one of the tables. "Come, my friend, come."

I stepped up onto the patio, admiring as I did so the floor's newly laid terrazzo tiles, and went over to where he sat.

"Well?"

I took the hand, pudgy, damp, which Andreas reached up to me. His eyes were gleaming behind his thick spectacles.

Excitement, pride, a swelling air of achievement, all were in that stare.

"What do you think? You may to speak honestly." And with a twist of his head he indicated the hotel and all around.

"Pumpkin to Golden Coach," I said. "It's a near miracle. I'd never have believed it possible."

Fleshy lips parted in a wide smile, Andreas said slowly, his voice shaking with emotion, "I tell you, my friend. Andreas, he may be a simple man, but he can do much. Anything is possible. Remember?" Then, motioning me to a seat beside him, he said, "You have just come from England? Then you must need refreshment. Please to sit and to take some food with your friend. Drink. Anything you want." He threw his arms wide then leant back in his seat. "You are my guest. What will you take?"

At that moment, dizzy as I was from the heat of the sun and the long hours of travel, I'd have liked more than anything to take a shower followed by a siesta, but it would have been churlish to spurn his eagerness to please. Besides, he was so obviously wanting my approval of all he'd accomplished that at very least I ought to toast his success. So, dropping into the chair beside his, I asked for a glass of wine, and Andreas called over his shoulder to a young man who stepped out of the shadows. "Mitsos, for Mister Peter, my good friend, you will bring wine and a plate of mezes."

"Mitsos is a good boy," Andreas said as the youth disappeared in the direction of the kitchen. "His family are poor islanders. So I give him work. They are grateful."

The smile that accompanied these words was one of genial complacency.

The food, fresh-cooked fish from the local boats, meat and vegetables from island farms, Andreas assured me, was as excellent as the honey-coloured retsina, and he was right. Tired though I was, I ate and drank well while I listened to Andreas tell me of what he had so far achieved at the Hotel Zeus and what there remained to do.

Every evening, I learnt, a guitarist came to the taverna to play and sing rembetika. "A very good musician, the island's best. You will hear him. The peoples from this village, they come to listen and to sing and dance. And others, too. They come. They all come." He paused. "To *my* hotel." His hands described a series of upward-moving circles, as though he was releasing doves into the air. "I tell you. Every night I make happen a celebration."

What more could anyone ask?

A beach, perhaps. That, too, had been created. Islanders had been employed to clean up the narrow strip to the harbour's right. Over several weeks, I was told, men laboured to remove the bigger rocks, convoys of lorries arrived to bury the pebbly strip beneath fresh sand, and, as I was to discover in the coming months, all day long the new-made beach was crowded with villagers as well as Andreas's paying guests, their sun-anointed bodies glistening along its tan stretch, their feet all pointing toward sea that lolled beyond their sun-loungers.

Whatever doubts might have lingered vanished like an Aegean dawn mist when I saw the beach. Andreas wasn't an empty-headed dreamer. I was even prepared to accept his explanation for why the design on the cover of all his menus showed, under the legend *ZEUS*, a naked, hirsute figure standing waist-deep in the sea, grasping a trident. The artist chosen for the work had, he said, remarked that to show Zeus with his customary thunderbolt might suggest the hotel was liable to uncertain weather, whereas a trident signified the bounty of the sea. Fair enough.

***

Given this, it wasn't so surprising that in the weeks that followed, I'd stroll down to the hotel for a drink after a morning's work, where Andreas, in his black suit no matter how hot the day, would join me, ordering wine (for me) and water for himself (he rarely allowed himself alcohol during the day); and there I'd listen to the further schemes he laid before me, schemes in which I came to believe almost as unquestioningly as he seemingly did.

There was for example, the roof garden. That summer, with the hotel fully booked most days, Andreas explained that he planned to turn the hotel's flat roof into a grassed-over area that would sport a cocktail bar and small orchestra. "So ladies can come in their high heels and dance," he said. "Not just nice ladies who stay here, but ladies from town, from all over the island.

From other islands. From Athens. *Everyone* will come to the Hotel Zeus." And when I asked how they were to get from port to the hotel, he said "I will arrange for taxis. Perhaps a hotel bus."

But, he said, his voice suddenly dropping from expansive delight to near-whispered entreaty as he leant across to me, he needed my assistance. Really? How could I possibly help him?

"I am a peasant, Mister Peter. No good school for Mister Andreas when he was a boy. I don't write proper. But you are a writer. I will pay you to prepare a brochure for me that can be put everywhere. Airports, international railway stations, embassies. I want you to use your best language. It will bring everyone to Andreas's hotel. Andreas the peasant."

He was, unusually for him, a little drunk. At all events I had never heard him before call himself a peasant. Simple, yes, peasant, no. But now, having used the term, joviality was replaced by a truculent look as he slammed his fist on the table and said, "A peasant maybe Andreas is. A fool, never."

Had the way I glanced at him provoked this outburst? If so, he quickly recovered himself. "You will help me?"

"Gladly," I said. "And you mustn't think of paying me. After all your hospitality, it will be a pleasure to do something for you."

He put a hand on my bare arm. It was clammy with sweat. "We understand each other," he said. "We are friends."

"We are friends," I told him.

"And I will pay you," he said. "That way we remain friends. Good friends."

A few days later he called to me as I walked up the lane from an early afternoon swim and invited me to sit at his table while he outlined a new plan.

"But first you must have a drink."

"A glass of water is all I need," I said.

Andreas looked disappointed. He wanted me to toast in wine his new plan. But never mind. Leaning toward me, he asked, as if in confidence, whether I had noticed the number of Japanese day trippers who came to the island.

How could I not? Day after day they were offloaded from cruise ships that stopped just long enough to allow for a quick visit by coach to the island's temple, followed by the obligatory stroll through the port town's narrow back streets and a meal at one or the other fish tavernas or ouzeries behind the fish market. After that, it was back to the ship and on to the next island.

Well, Andreas said, a taverna very near the port was about to become available. The owner was selling up, and he, Andreas, intended to buy it and install a Chinese chef to serve Chinese food. "You understand what I say? The Japanese, they will see my taverna before they see any other and they will come to me." He paused, waiting for my agreement, my acknowledgement of yet another masterstroke in the making.

What to say? Tentatively, I suggested that it might make better sense to appoint a Japanese chef who would know about Japanese cuisine, but Andreas waved my words away. "Rice. Fish," he said. "It is all the same."

As he made this announcement we were joined by a middle-aged woman whom I'd seen not long before on the beach where, shoe-horned into a fashionably-cut black swimsuit that made no attempt to hide her Rubenesque curves, she lay broiling on a lounger. Now, wrapped in a loose, blue-and-green chiffon dress, she was drawing out a chair as Andreas, sweating in his black suit, stood to kiss her on both cheeks.

"This is Anne," he said to me, and then, a certain hesitancy in his smile, he turned to her. "Anne, please to meet my good friend, Mister Peter. He is from England."

We shook hands, and I noticed the pale pink of her painted fingernails and the jewel-encrusted gold rings that puffed up the flesh of her middle fingers.

"Anywhere in particular?"

"The Midlands," I said.

"Essex, me. An original Essex girl."

"I guessed."

"And can you guess *who* I am?"

"Anne is my wife," Andreas said, looking at me, then quickly at her.

But she ignored his look. "One of them," she said, laughing, as she reached in her expensive-looking leather handbag for a cigarette. "The first, actually. He got three children out of me, didn't you, pet. Then he met Lady Jane."

Soon after my arrival that summer, as Andreas and I sat over a lunchtime drink, I'd asked after Jane, realising that I hadn't seen her, hadn't heard her voice, its manicured vowels so unlike Andreas's croaky gutturals. Was she well? Was one or more of the children requiring her presence in England?

"She does not like the heat," Andreas had told me. "Jane will come in the autumn." At the time, the explanation had seemed plausible enough.

Perhaps wanting to put me at my ease, Anne said, "She knows about me, no probs. Like I know about her. We get on alright, the three of us, don't we, Andy? She's good for his business, see, touch of class, and he's good for her. Puts his hand in his pocket and out comes a bunch of readies for her to spend on fancy china and horse-riding for the kiddies. All four of them. Plus my three. What a good boy he is. Takes care of us all. Father to the nation, aren't you, my old precious?"

Her voice held no trace of resentment. It was as though she was amused by him, no worse.

She offered us cigarettes and, when we refused, said as she lit one for herself, "Oh, well, we all have different vices. Andy doesn't have many, though he's sometimes a bit too fond of the ladies. Not that he means any harm. Him and me are sort of divorced, and her and him are sort of married. And I get to spend the summer here, which is several up on Clacton, I don't mind telling you."

If at first he'd seemed discomforted by Anne's appearance, Andreas had by now quite lost his wary look. He beamed at us both. "I was telling Mister Peter about my plan to open a Chinese taverna," he said.

"And I hope you told him to drop it," she said to me, before tilting up her head to blow smoke toward the electric fan that flapped ineffectually above us. "Bloody silly idea." She lowered her gaze, smiled at Andreas. "You might get some change out of a take-away, though I wouldn't bank on it, but a Chinese taverna.... Andy, old love, your brains must be melting in the sun." She leant across and patted him affectionately on the cheek.

He winked at me. "She is no business woman" he said, "but she will like the profits."

Still, in the days that followed no more was said about the proposal for a Chinese taverna, and although I handed over a draft brochure for the roof-top garden cum cocktail bar, Andreas put it to one side without even glancing at it. Nor, I noticed, did he repeat his earlier offer to pay me for my work. By then he was more interested in a scheme to have the ceilings of the hotel painted in what he called "Classic style. Gods, wars, scenes from our history. If you know of an artist who can do this work, tell me. I will pay good money. And of course to do this work, it will make him famous." I think there was even mention of a private jet in which the artist, should he or she happen to live outside Greece, could be flown to Athens. Of the golf course and hospital that had so preoccupied him when we first met there was no mention, and I didn't think it a good idea to bring the subject up. It was, I thought, obvious that Andreas had seen sense.

***

It must have been a few weeks after Anne had packed up and returned to England and there was still no sign of Jane that the whispers began. My intendedly brief visit to Leros in fact stretched out so that a full month passed before I got back to the island, late one night in mid-to-late September.

The following morning, early, I went into town to shop, and afterward stopped off at a waterside bar. That was where I heard the first rumours, mutterings about unpaid workers at Hotel Zeus, of unsettled bills, of tradesmen left out of pocket for goods and labour supplied.

Like all islands, ours was always full of rumours, many of them not much more than malicious gossip, and at first I tried to shrug them off. Less easy to shrug off was the evidence of my own eyes. Strolling down past the hotel for a swim that afternoon, I noticed that the patio no longer looked spotlessly clean, and when, later, having sat for a while on the now more or less deserted beach, I went into the hotel for an ouzo, I saw piles of bedding in the lobby. It was late in the season so perhaps the absence of guests wasn't a big surprise, but when, a few days afterward I ate at the taverna, I was disappointed by how little choice of food there was and, even more, by its poor quality. It was stale, greasy, badly cooked.

Why? What was going on? I wanted to ask Andreas, but he wasn't there and I realised that I hadn't once seen him since getting back from Leros. There had been trouble with the chef, Mitsos the waiter told me as he cleared my plate away and brought another half-carafe of retsina, looking uncomfortable as he spoke.

And Andreas? Where was Andreas?

"He is away on business. I hope he will be back for the weekend."

***

But he wasn't. Nor was there any sign of the guitarist who earlier in the summer had played and sung to appreciative listeners. Only a few people gathered at tables on that Saturday night, and as though in sympathy with the mood of uncertain, almost sullen temper, the sky darkened for an approaching storm which broke violently over our heads mid-evening. Wind and rain stirred up the water in the little harbour, boats strained and creaked at their moorings, and, retreating from the rain-lashed taverna into the hotel itself, we watched as the banner *HOTEL ZEUS WELCOMES YOU* was ripped away by a violent gust and flung into the road where it lay while cars, groping through the dark on their way back to town, ran over it with a soft swoosh as though squeezing the last breath of air from some brought-to-earth dirigible.

Two days later I closed the flat for winter and flew back to England.

***

And now, here in the spring of 1995, I was back on the island, finishing my ouzo as I stared at the ocean-going *JULIET* and understood that it was being loaded with valuables from the hotel of which Andreas had claimed the proud ownership but from which he had perhaps fled in ignominy, unless worse had happened to him.

My earlier elation when I saw the hotel open had, after my meeting with Big John and his henchmen, changed to one of foreboding. The few people who might have known of Andreas's whereabouts all shrugged or shook their heads when I asked them about him. I suspected that one or two knew more than they let on, but as nobody admitted to having any information—some even pretended they couldn't remember who he was—"Oh, *that* Andreas, no, he left the island a long time ago, surely"—their feigned ignorance only deepened my concern for him.

After returning from town along the back road—preferable to the coast road not only because it was prettier but because, at this time of year in particular, it was barely used by cars—I spent some time storing the food I'd bought, then opened all the doors and windows and, in approved Greek fashion, draped my rugs over the verandah before sweeping out the flat, thinking as I did so about the three who'd commandeered the hotel when I'd dropped by, hoping to see Andreas. And what I chiefly thought was not merely were they up to no good—that much was obvious and the boss was, as the saying goes, someone you wouldn't want to bump into on a dark night—but that their presence in the *Zeus* suggested that something bad must have happened to Andreas. Like bailiff's men, Big John and his two henchmen were there to remove the hotel's contents. But they weren't bailiff's men. Asset strippers, then? Or, to put it more plainly, crooks.

I finished tidying the flat, relaid the rugs, closed the windows and then thought I might as well wander down to the waterfront. One of the fishermen there might possibly know something about Andreas or the trio who had been and by now no doubt left.

But to my surprise the entrance door to the hotel was still open and the four-wheel drive was parked out front. As I stood looking at it, the man called Trevor emerged, bandy-legged with the weight of the carton he was carrying.

"Wotcher," he said, grinning as he staggered towards me.

"I thought you'd be gone by now."

"Nah. Bit like a bad smell, eh. We're difficult to get rid of."

I watched as, pulling and pushing at the pile of boxes already cluttering the Chelsea tractor, he eventually found space for the one he had brought out.

"Right," he said. "That's your lot, Juliet."

Then he turned to me. "Fancy a beer?" The enquiry seemed genuine.

"Won't I be interrupting your work?"

"All done and dusted," he said. "Soon as Big John and Wave are back we'll be shot of here."

I followed him into the hotel lobby and waited while he dug bottles out of a cool bag beside the table at which he motioned me to sit.

We clinked bottles and drank.

"So where are the others?"

"Gone into town. Bit of business to attend to." And before I could even think to ask what business Big John might be up to, Trevor said, "Not much of a town, like I said earlier."

"I like it."

Perhaps sensing the resentment in my voice—how dare anyone criticise the island—he said, grinning, "No offence. But there's not a lot doing, is there? I mean, we've been here three days, had time to look the place over, drove this way and that, ain't seen anything worth stopping for. I wouldn't give you a three-pound note for it. Straight up. No real class. Not a Merc or a Jag in sight. I ain't had a prawn cocktail or decent steak since I've been here. I reckon it's a dump. Good enough for Andreas, though."

He grinned affably.

So what did he think was class? Obvious. Flash cars, villas with pools, hostess bars. Trevor must have found his El Dorado in Costa del Crime.

As though to confirm my suspicion, like the word—or thought—made flesh, Big John materialised in the lobby. He had entered noiselessly but now he said to Trevor, "If you're all done here you can go and get your bag. Wave and me are ready packed. I'll finish your beer."

The words were levelly spoken, but there was no doubt who was in control, and it wasn't Trevor.

"OK boss," the small man said, levering himself up. I shook the hand he held out to me. "Nice meeting you," I said, "safe journey."

He looked, I thought, startled, but left the lobby without saying another word.

Big John took Trevor's place opposite me and, having used a handkerchief to wipe the neck of the bottle the other had barely started, raised it to me and silently drank.

Then he said, studying the bottle before he let his eyes fix on mine. "Spot of bother earlier on as you probably gathered."

"Oh?"

"Yeh. Trevor got some unwelcome news from home. Seemed my kids, who'd been looking after the house while I've been away, weren't quite ready for my return. But they are now. All sorted."

"Have you been on holiday?"

The smile was there and then in an instant gone again. "Sort of. Been out of England for a few years. Business matters."

"And business brought you to the island?"

"You could say that." He looked around the lobby, studied the ceiling, then brought his eyes level with mine. "Andreas's business, chiefly."

"I was wondering," I said, "how you know Andreas."

Big John said, "Me and Andreas go back a long way. He was married to my sister, see."

I did, or thought I did. "Anne?"

"You met her then?" He didn't seem surprised. "Yes, Anne. Nice old-fashioned girl. From Billericay. Andreas was a bit of a naughty boy, the way he treated her."

"I'm surprised," I said, "very surprised. She certainly seemed happy enough when I saw her at the hotel here last summer. I'd have said that she and Andreas got on well together. I know their relationship was—well, irregular—but they seemed genuinely fond of each other. She knew about Andreas's other relationships, you know."

Big John picked at the label on his beer bottle. Using first finger and thumb to roll into a pellet the piece he'd scratched away, he flicked it across the lobby. Then he said, "I don't give a monkey's who he screws, though it beats me what any woman sees in him, especially that West End bint he took up with. But he got Anne into trouble, did you know that?"

I shook my head, puzzled. His words made no sense. From all I could recall, there seemed no history of trouble between Anne and Andreas, and supposing there had once been—over Lady Jane, say—she had surely long since forgiven him.

"How did he get your sister into trouble?" I asked. "If you don't mind talking about it, that is."

"No, I don't *mind*." The mimicry was accompanied by a thin smile. "Might do you good to hear, just so you don't get all soft-hearted about dear old Andreas." He took a swig of his beer, set the bottle down and said, "When he left here last summer, our Andy—that was her name for him, Randy Andy—he gave Anne some parcels to take back to England. A friend will be waiting at Heathrow to collect them from you, my dear, no need to know what's in them." He paused, looked keenly at me. "But what do you know, when she gets to Heathrow it isn't a friend who's waiting, it's Customs. They want to look through her luggage and 'Well, well, well, what have we here? Now this *is* a surprise.' And before you can say knife she's in court on a charge of drug-running. Took me a heap of dosh to get her off that."

"You hired a smart lawyer?"

The laugh was without warmth. "Do me a favour. Let's just say I got friends who know how to lose evidence. Confuse reports. Muddy clear waters. So Anne's alright." He leant closer. "But she might not have been. See, Andreas has form. She hasn't, but nobody wants to know that. And right now she doesn't want to know Andreas."

I thought about what I had heard and thought, reluctantly, that it made sense. "So you think Andreas heard about Anne's being arrested and decided to vanish before anyone came looking for him."

Big John's eyes flickered then became blank. "I think that's what he *tried* to do. Yes." He drained the last of his beer and stood up. "Well, business calls. I don't suppose we'll meet again."

I, too, got to my feet and shook the hand he extended.

Then I left.

I didn't though go up the lane. Instead, I decided to walk into town by the coast road. I needed to think over all I'd been told, to try to reconcile my Andreas with the petty or not so petty crook who had put his former wife in danger and, as a consequence, almost certainly brought greater danger on himself. "I think that's what he *tried* to do." The cool manner in which those words had been uttered suggested that Andreas's attempt to escape may have ended in failure. And if so, that could mean only one thing. Andreas was dead.

I was brooding on this dark likelihood as I rounded the headland from where the town came into view across the blue waters of the bay. The view was partly obscured by the same large, ocean-going yacht I'd seen earlier that day. It was riding at anchor some way out from the shore, its engine idling, one or two crew members in their white ducks leaning over the side, smoking and laughing. They were presumably waiting for orders to weigh anchor. Millionaires cruised the summer Mediterranean in such yachts, each trying to outdo the other in the elegance, size, and speed of their boats, to say nothing of the presumed enviability of their guest-lists. But this yacht had no guest list, though it was conceivable that its owner was a millionaire and bound for southern Spain.

***

It had gone by the time, once more taking the coast road, I returned from town later that evening. And as for the ugly, unlit hotel looming up at a bend in the road by the little harbour, I sensed as I walked toward it that it must now be empty. Stepping up onto the patio where the previous year I had so often sat and talked, I tried to peer through the locked front door but shutters had been pulled across and I could see nothing but my own face dimly reflected in the door's glass panes.

***

Over the following months my few enquiries about Andreas were either greeted with shrugs of indifference or, sometimes, though rarely, explosions of anger. Andreas? You mean that bastard crook who went off with our money. No, nobody knows where he is. Find and bring him to us and you'll be doing us a favour. But as time went on so anger shaded into contempt. Andreas? That peasant. And then contempt faded into indifference. Andreas? Oh, him. Who cares. He was last year's news. As for the hotel, like other abandoned hotels scattered around the island, all of them built in the anticipation of wealth and glory which in the course of years turned to ruin, it began to settle back into its former state of neglect and gathering decrepitude, and in the years that followed it remained shut. The family who were said to be its owners never visited the island

and in their absence nobody else offered to take over the running of *Hotel Zeus*.

Some years after Andreas's disappearance, a rumour spread about someone who claimed to know someone else who had heard that Andreas, far from being dead, was now running a hotel in Venice. Or was it Verona? Or Vienna? Or Valencia? Or Vancouver? Valparaiso? Ventura? Veracruz? The Greeks know their ports. They also know how to use laughter as a needle to deflate pretension. And perhaps Andreas, with his absurdly expansive dreams, deserved to be laughed at. To that extent at least the islanders could avenge themselves on the man whose airy visions had cost them money and goods they had no hope of recovering. Laughter was their only pay-back.

Nobody likes to be taken for a fool, and Andreas had made fools of quite a few of the islanders. As he'd made a fool of me. And yet I couldn't bring myself to think of him as a cynical manipulator, out for his own ends. A part of him, I'm sure, really believed in his dreamt-of role as a kind of benevolent lord of the island. Vain though he may have been, he wanted to be admired for deeds of public charity. Somewhere within that swarthy, stocky man, was a dream not merely of making money but of doing good. Yet he must also have sensed or feared that underneath every grateful expression lurked a contemptuous smirk. What, after all, *was* he? He knew the answer well enough. He was a peasant.

I think now that this was what caused his explosions of rage. In his summer of success it wasn't unusual to see him at his table sharing drinks or a meal with another man or a group of men, heads together in what looked to be conspiratorial discussion. They were rarely the same, these men, though they were of a type: sharp white trousers crammed into fleshy buttocks and thighs, dark polo shirts from the open necks of which gouts of chest hair foamed, much gold at neck and wrist. They smoked continuously and sipped ouzo or whisky while Andreas listened to whatever they were telling him, staring steadily at them and from time to time nodding or, perhaps, jerking his head backward in an emphatic no. They were presumably trying to get him to buy into some plan that would, so the pitch went, make them all oodles of money.

And then, quite suddenly, Andreas's mood would change.

"*Malakas*." As he roared out the word his hand would smash down open palm on the table, and that would be the end of the *tête-à-tête*. The others would rise with as much grace as they could manage and saunter away, leaving him to glare after them.

Although I never knew what the discussions were about, I was instinctively on his side. Under that coarse, sun-roughened appearance, that peasant in the ill-fitting black suit, was a thin-skinned man, quick to feel resentment, liable to detect an insult even where none was intended, but shrewd enough to be on his guard against those he had good reason to suspect couldn't be trusted. I think he came to trust me. After all I didn't want anything from him. And I understood that for him business at its best was to all intents and purposes a form of barter. I give *you* something, you give *me* something. I supply you with wine or beer, you write me a brochure. Even the grandest dreams were forms of barter. You bring me your illness. I supply you with a hospital.

"A simple Greek peasant" used to be a phrase dear to tourist guides. You hear it less often nowadays though it still comes from the pens or lips of some. Well, *malakas* to that. There was nothing simple about Andreas. He was shrewd in the dictionary sense: astute and penetrating. And beneath the joviality, the bonhomie, were depths I could only glimpse, incalculable meanings and implications I would never understand.

Yet in the end he didn't prove wily enough. Astute as he undoubtedly was, he must, Icarus-like, have flown too high and then plummeted to destruction. Poor Andreas. A crook, but not by any means a bad man. And a puzzle, too, a mystery I would never resolve.

Until, that is, one day in the summer of 2001. It was then, sitting on the balcony of my flat overlooking the lane down to the Hotel Zeus, that I began to read Italo Calvino's *Difficult Loves*, and in the last story of this early collection by a writer I revere, I came, if not face to face with Andreas, then certainly with someone very like him.

"A Plunge Into Real Estate" is about a Milanese called Quinto who yearns to follow the city fashion for building apartment blocks by the sea. He decides to erect his own block on land his mother owns. He will then rent out the apartments at a sizeable profit. Unfortunately, Quinto is short of money. He needs a builder prepared to work on the cheap. "Then Caisotti showed up." This brief, laconic sentence introduces a man whom a friend of Quinto's tells him is "quite uncouth... he can scarcely speak Italian". The archetypal peasant. Caisotti agrees to the terms Quinto offers him.

From the start, things go wrong. The workers Caisotti employs fail to appear. Why, Quinto asks? Because, Caisotti explains, he can't afford to pay them. There's a cash flow problem. But why should there be such a problem, Quinto wants to know. He has already given the builder money. Yes, but it isn't enough to cover building materials, and Caisotti therefore needs to obtain credit from bankers and tradesmen, who won't let him have it, and without credit the money that should go on wages has to be spent on cement and tools. Caisotti's explanations and excuses for delays, the non-appearance of workers and materials, become increasingly tortuous or, you could say, shrewdly plausible, and culminate in a scene where Quinto, trying to take the work away from Caisotti, summons him to a meeting at a lawyer's office. This is how Calvino describes it.

"As Caisotti came into the office (the atmosphere of the place was presumably calculated to intimidate him) and saw all those educated people writing away, he looked around like a trapped animal who instinctively tries to escape but knows it's no longer any use."

Yet by the end of the meeting Caisotti has managed not only to keep his job but to discompose and outwit those lined up against him.

Just like Andreas, I thought, remembering a moment when I'd come across him at a café in town, arguing with an English estate agent who lived and worked on the island, and from whose lips I had sometime earlier heard tell of "simple Greek peasants"—the words accompanied by a smile of great complacency. But Andreas ripped a hole in this smug carapace. He had apparently rented from the agent holiday flats near his hotel. They were to serve as an overflow for when the Zeus was fully booked, but as this didn't happen he never paid any rent.

"But you took possession of the flats, and so I couldn't rent them to visitors at a time when the island was full." The agent's voice rose in exasperated self-righteousness. "I lost good money, money you now owe me."

"That's not how I remember our arrangement" Andreas said. He was calm, unmoved. And he wasn't going to pay.

Arrangement. Not contract. As always with Andreas, nothing was ever written down. Ah, the simple peasant. Simple Caisotti, able to turn the tables on the lawyer and his smart friends. Calvino's description of his peasant builder might, a few details apart, have been of the man I knew. Caisotti's "big, fleshy face seemed made of stuff too formless to retain its lineaments or expressions; they at once tended to subside as though engulfed not so much by the deep folds at the corners of his eyes and mouth, but by the sandy, porous texture of his whole face." As for Caisotti's snub nose: Calvino provides a detailed account of the "unusual distance between his nostrils and his upper lip, which made him look either stupid or brutal," while the thick lips that "disappeared altogether at the corners," give him "the look of a shark, a suggestion heightened by the slightly receding chin above the broad throat." An unflattering account, to be sure, but we are seeing Caisotti through the eyes of a man who at first condescends to him, then despises him, then is outraged by him, and is at the last humiliatingly outwitted by the Italian peasant, and all without our ever quite knowing whether from the outset Caisotti intended the final outcome or has simply got lucky. The story ends with Caisotti and his wife installed as legal owners of the block of flats built entirely at his employer's expense. Devilish cunning? Or has he simply—ha—taken advantage of the chances that come his way, chances for the most part created by the miscalculations and blunders of his "betters".

Simple Caisotti. Simple Andreas. But comparisons only go so far. Caisotti ends as a success. I'd like to believe that somewhere Andreas is alive and carrying on business. I doubt it, though. More probably he's dead, bumped off by crooks who were more ruthless than he was, less troubled by dreams.

***

There is a coda to all this. As I never saw Andreas again, so I never saw the trio of heavies who had been emptying the Hotel

Zeus that late March morning in 1995. But I may have read about them. Not long ago I was leafing through the morning's newspaper when the following headline caught my eye.

Pair jailed for 'Essex Boys' murders win the right to appeal.

Underneath was an account of how a judge had referred back to the Court of Appeal the sentencing in 1998 of Michael Steele and Jack Whomes, for the "murders of Pat Tate, Tony Tucker and Craig Rolfe in what became known as the Essex Boys killings. The three were shot dead in a Range Rover parked in a country lane in Rettendon, Essex, in December 1995." The report went on to explain that the murder of the three men was the culmination of a feud between rival gangs about "a shipment of poor-quality cannabis."

Reading those words, I thought back to my certainty that the ocean-going yacht, *JULIET*, which brought Big John, Trevor and Waverley from Spain to our island was being loaded with goods from the Hotel Zeus before returning there, or—why not, I thought now—heading for the Essex coast. "A feud between rival gangs." What did that remind me of? Of course. Big John's remark about the spot of bother with his kids who weren't looking after his interests. And then I remembered the same man, whatever his real name might be—Pat? Tony? Craig?—mentioning Billericay as a place he might have to visit. And Anne had mentioned Clacton.

I got out my atlas. England. The south of England. Yes, there Billericay was. And there, some ten miles east, was Rettendon, just above the River Crouch and, as house agents like to say, conveniently situated for access to the Essex coast. And Clacton wasn't far off, either. Anne was Big John's sister. Suppose she'd been caught ferrying drugs for Andreas and suppose that behind Andreas's request for her to help him out was a drugs baron to whom he owed money? Suppose, even, that the baron and Big John were one and the same? Too many supposes, I know, too many loose ends. Too little to convince me that "the Essex Boys" were the three men I'd inadvertently encountered as they were in the act of cleaning out the Hotel Zeus.

But as Andreas himself had said, anything is possible.